I

THE END OF THE TRAIL
A 100 MILE RUNNING ODYSSEY

By

JOHN DAVID FISCHER

A long distance runner of average ability looks back 20 years at his taking on the challenge of racing the Western States 100 Mile Endurance Run.

Published by:

John David Fischer
2306 S. Memory St.
Visalia, California 93277

First Printing, June 2006

ISBN 0-9779911-0-5

Copyright © 2006 By John David Fischer
Printed in the United States by
Jostens Commercial Printing
Visalia, California
www.jostens.com/commercial

Cover design and book digital preparation by
Dick Tristao's TwoBitGrafix
Visalia, California
twobitgrafix@comcast.net

For information on ordering a book or bulk purchases you may contact
the author at his address above or email him at
jdfrun@aol.com

DEDICATION:

To my parents, Sid and Ellen Fischer, two enthusiastic
and kind, beautiful people who always encouraged me
to go wherever my dreams might take me

ODYSSEY:

A long journey or voyage marked by many changes of
fortune; an intellectual or spiritual wandering or quest.

Other books by John David Fischer

The Cowhide: A High School Football Tradition

PROLOGUE

As I push my once strong legs down the gentle duff-covered path in an alternate rhythm of power walking and easy jogging, I glance upwards at the huge red-barked cathedrals of giant Sequoias that align that path, their majestic presences softly soothing my sometimes restless spirit. The trail is one of my favorites, a place where year after year I return to arouse and contemplate my favorite life memories, visions of many years past when I was young and carefree and could glide effortlessly across the trails toward destinations that were often unknown and unyielding.

Those trails of life memories have been sometimes good and sometimes less than desirable, but I know that at all times they presented some unique challenges in this game of life as it is. If I fell down, I scrambled back up and continued on. If I encountered a rare moment of unknown energy and the euphoria of living life on the brink, I let the flow come to me and didn't question why. I floated down that path on wings of delight and let the winds of the heavens carry me onward at breakneck speed until the path became rugged and rocky again and then I slowed down.

Never did I stop running forward in some fashion, through all the highs and lows that life presented me. My trail of life has been like the trail I now embark upon, a trail with all its undulations, all its diversity, with its roots and snags ready to reach up and trip me, with its soft, needle covered carpet, inviting me to gently glide while my mind races forward to contemplate all that life itself reveals to me.

At the age of 63 I realize with a certain finality that I have traveled a long distance down that trail, and that somewhere off in the hazy future is the end of the journey, that place where the path suddenly just stops, with nowhere else to go. Somewhere is the finish line of that trail, the place where I can finally rest and go off into the sunset and experience some kind of new challenge of the spirit that all of us eventually encounter.

In my younger days, my legs and youthful energy carried me on an unending adventure, racing at breakneck speed down my trail of life. Today the legs and the body are still willing to embrace those same experiences, but somehow they don't respond with the same vitality that was once present in the past. Yet the spirit is still there, the spirit that embraces what it is able to hold, even as the physical limitations continue to diminish.

Twenty years ago I had reached the highlight and peak as a long distance runner. I had started running a few years earlier and ran my races on the roads and the trails in the spirit of inner competition within myself, trying to improve each time I took on a new challenge. At some point I reached the pinnacle of my racing prowess just at about the time I reached the same pinnacle of my life force and energy. Somewhere my race was half over and began the final stretch run toward the finish line.

During the peak of my racing long distances I took on a challenge that today seems like some kind of crazy dream. At the time it somewhat frightened me because in my mind and heart, I didn't really believe at first that it was possible for an average person to accomplish. I decided to run a 100 mile race over the high Sierra Nevada mountain range on trails. My simple goal was to try to finish the Western States 100 Mile Endurance Run from Squaw Valley to Auburn before the 30 hour time limit, with the outside possibility of making the entire distance in one day, 24 hours.

The Western States 100 is probably the best known long distance event in the world of ultramarathons. It is held near the end of June each year and traverses trails and dirt roads across one of the most majestic mountain ranges in the country. Over the years thousands have run the course, many more than once. Hundreds of average runners have taken on the challenge.

Twenty years ago after months of intense preparation and training, I also took on the challenge of the Western States. When I took off from the starting line early that summer morning, I had been a runner for less than five years and hadn't originally intended to take on such a huge engagement. The story of my trek is not much different from the many others who have run the course. In fact, my story may be more common among ultrarunners than the exception. I'm sure the account of the race will conjure up many memories of others who have done the race over the many years.

For those who have never done the race or are thinking about doing it, I am about to take you with me out on that trail for the full 100 miles, revealing to you my hopes, fears, highs and lows, pain, ecstacy, and my inner thoughts as I make my way across the mountains. You will come along in my footsteps as my race progresses from the first step to the finishing banner. The varied observations of the journey are taken from a detailed diary written within the first two weeks after completing the race. At the end of each chapter I offer to you some current observations about my life leading up to the race or those journeys that followed.

At the end of the journey I will discuss those things that I did to prepare myself for the race. I will not only talk about the physical preparation, but also the mental aspect of taking on such a challenge. I will discuss in detail the training methods I used twenty years ago. I offer such advice with the understanding that I'm not an expert on the subject. At the time I was an experiment of one, but somehow I came up with a program that worked for me.

One year prior to my quest, I was a pacer for another runner. For the next two years after the race, I paced other runners on the course, both unsuccessfully. Three years after the race, I attempted and completed the race for a second time. Before the entire adventure was all over I had run 74 races of a marathon distance or longer.

Today, twenty years later, the race is still clear in my mind as a defining moment in my life, a challenge which resulted in an ending that has affected my life in a powerful way, a finish that taught me that life is full of challenges and that as human beings we must not sit back and ignore them or reject them because they are too difficult. In this moment of one fateful day I reached the end of the trail, and I have discovered that we all have long trails to run, but that the endings of those trails keep beckoning for us to reach further and further, that we never stop because we believe we are at the end.

When we finally reach the ending of that final trail, we reach the end of our lives as we know it on earth. As we get closer to that ending, we look for other trails. The challenges may be of a more gentle nature, whether it is hiking parts of those same trails we used to run, walking slowly in a meadow of wild flowers, watching children play, or observing a small spider build its intricate web on a bush in the fading reflection of a sunset.

Please join with me on my personal quest as I take you on my physical and spiritual journey of 100 miles on my special trail.

THE END OF THE TRAIL

In 1979 John David Fischer decides to take up running to lose weight and get in shape. He runs his first race, a four miler, in 1980. Just six years later he decides to challenge the Western States 100 Mile Endurance Run, the country's most well-known ultra endurance running event, a race run over the Sierra Nevada mountain range from the Squaw Valley ski area to the town of Auburn in California.

After months of intense training, he toes the starting line on June, 1986, at the age of 43 in an attempt to finish the course. An average runner, Fischer has many doubts about completing the course. This story takes the reader literally step by step through every section of his race toward his destiny with the finish line. You will relive his high and lows points during the race, the physical and mental obstacles he faces, and his thoughts about the race and life as he runs on the trail.

Along the way you will discover what he learns about himself and how it has affected his life during the past twenty years. The many hours he spends during the day and nighttime hours is a memorable experience, one of great determination to reach the finish line. As he approaches the end of the race, he realizes the journey on the trail has become a metaphor for his own life's journey.

X

TABLE OF CONTENTS

CHAPTER 1
THE STARTING LINE

What have those lonely mountains worth revealing?
More glory and more grief than I can tell;
The earth that wakes one human heart to feeling
Can center both the worlds of Heaven and Hell.
(Emily Bronte)

June 28, 1986

The blaring, penetration of the television floodlights blinds me as I mingle in the crowded company of other runners, most strapping on waists belts (also called fanny packs), checking liquid supplies in plastic bottles, and giving out quiet, friendly good lucks and farewells to other runners. Non-running friends join in a subdued celebration at the start of this magnificent endurance event, snapping pictures, checking their runners' supplies, receiving and giving last minute instructions, and wishing their runners good fortune in the trek ahead. The noise is a low-pitched but loud, penetrating mumble, a mumble of fear mixed with half-sure confidence. It is the last bit of community conversation before the runners are left to be on their own.

The runners' garb is a kaleidoscope of colors and style, punctuated by the domination of the color white mixed with smatterings of all the other colors of the rainbow. Some runners wear long sleeve T-shirts to cut the nippy, high-mountain, early morning summer breeze. Some of the braver ones wear short sleeve T-shirts or even singlets. Others put their short sleeve shirts on as second layers over their long sleeve ones.

Most runners wear hats; there are long bills, short bills, and no bills; some have sun reflective nets hanging on their hats draped across their necks. Each runner brings a unique, individualistic, but practical color of white, the sun-reflective brightness that will protect him from the burning brutality of the sun's rays as the long, summer daylight hours

1

drone on to their completion with the arrival of the blackened night many hours down the trail.

The clock imperceptibly ticks down to the five o'clock hour, only minutes away now, and from a silent, invisible signal picked up by the gathered masses, the quiet roar picks up an octave. The non-running friends begin to slowly drop out of the group, leaving only the warriors on center stage, searching through the sea of brightness for some sign to begin the attack.

I find myself standing next to my friend Roger, and we wish each other one last farewell. Suddenly the runners ahead of me stride quickly forward in a darting, urgent but short stampede and stop in front of the starting banner and momentarily halt behind the race officials to wait for the starting gun. The roar of anticipation soars, and from my place back in the middle I glance to the side and then behind me. In the tight pack my running friends are now blurs, like so many rocks in a sun-reflecting stream, their faces pointed ahead in eager anticipation, ready to react in a stampede to the leader of the herd. I adjust my glasses and try to focus on my surroundings.

I observe many people and unfamiliar faces outlined in shadows standing above me on the bank of rocks to my left, lips silently moving and eyes brightly anticipating. Figures are blurred by the intensity of the beams of television lights. I glance to the front again into the blinding bank of lights just ahead and above the starting banner. I am part of the cast on this center stage, ready to unite with the others in the performances of our lives. My body is relaxed, but my heart is beating rapidly and strongly. I can almost feel hundreds of other hearts also slamming against heaving chests. I take a deep breath, but I feel like a spectator viewing my own body in a mass of quivering energy.

For several years now, and most recently during the last seven months, I have been anticipating this moment, reliving it in my conscious and unconscious fantasies, perceiving it so far off and impossible that I just know race day won't ever arrive. I can't really be doing this race, I have apprised myself over and over during the past few months. My fantasies are about to become factual, the reality of an adventure that I cannot ever envision or anticipate I will survive and endure. This can't really be happening. No one will really fire that gun; someone please tell me I won't be able to go out with the others on this daring journey into the unknown.

The moment is really upon me, but I know that in the actuality of the situation, I am still dreaming. The dazzling lights blur out all sense of reality. The spectators are statues on their bases of stone. I am alive, but all the others around me are only figments of my racing and panicking mind.

The crowded body noise rises now to the breaking point. My ears feel the tightness and tenseness of the sound to the point of nearly shattering. My eyes are blurry; tears drip from my eyes from the burning glare of the lights. I know the moment is at hand. The seconds stand still as time stops suddenly and abruptly, and a new crescendo of noiseless air pressure fills my ears and my head, ready to explode. My blood is no longer flowing, frozen in my veins and arteries. Conscious feeling is gone from my muscles, joints, and nerves. I look out and see the scene before me, but my body has melted beyond any sensation.

Quiet air tension is suddenly shattered by the startling, muffled blast from a shotgun, and the pressure explodes from my dream and runs down to the earth, meeting reality in my feet. My journey has commenced, a voyage of anticipation for the past eternity. I now am joined in soul with 414 other individuals battling the same war, not a war against a seen enemy, but a secret battle of our souls against unseen soul-destroying demons, each of us united permanently with the others, yet each drawing upon individual will and gut desire to begin and finish the journey. I pick up my foot and take a tentative first step among the thousands that will follow in my search for the silver lining at the end of this endless trail.

The start is chaotic as runners gather behind the starting banner.

I am an ultrarunner, and I have begun the longest, most difficult expedition of my life, my journey over the mountains, through canyons, dust, water, lightness and darkness, over well-worn trails and dirt roads, thrusting through physical and mental pain, trying to ascertain the sunlight of joy at the end of the journey. I have started my 100 mile journey of my first Western States Endurance Run from Squaw Valley near Lake Tahoe to the little town of Auburn on Interstate Highway 80, some 35 miles northeast of Sacramento, California.

I invite you to take a trip with me 100 miles on the most beautiful, soul-searching journey I will ever undertake. Come join me in my 100 mile odyssey across the Sierras.

It is now exactly 20 years later in the summer of 2006 and my aging body can no longer even think of doing such a race. It is all I can do to participate in an occasional race of walking and jogging of no more than a 10K, usually opting for a shorter two miler if it is offered. However, I still can participate fully in a lot of fairly strenuous physical activities, certainly more than 90 percent of the people of my age.

More important my mental and spiritual being is still strong and steady, ready to take on each new and delightful challenge that life may offer. One thing that race way back in the summer of 1986 me taught was that I can face any new challenge presented to me. I can meet both the successes and defeats of life head on and come away with only temporary bruises. Just as the race was a journey of ups and downs, my life journey since then has faced the same undulations, and I find that I am still trucking onward toward the finishing line of life.

My challenges now tend more toward the intellectual, those that engage my mind in long endurance runs of thought and contemplation. I also can still take on physical challenges of a less demanding nature. Instead of running, I can take a hike on the same trails, slowing down to take in all the side pleasures that I missed when my main goal was to reach a finish line. Now my main goal is to enjoy the journey more than I did before. I also can engage in other sporting pursuits, among them alpine skiing, where my old endurance still kicks in to enjoy a beautiful sport that I first learned back the 1950's.

I do what I can do now in my life and I don't look back. I make adjustments and throw out the old pursuits that I can no longer do and add new ones that I can still accomplish.

CHAPTER 2
OFF TO EMIGRANT PASS
(4.7 MILES)

Great visions often start
With small dreams.
(Saying)

The initial feeling I encounter as I get out of the car near the start is one of panic. Bright, glaring floodlights greet my eyes, blurring out all my feelings of the actual physical presence of other people. After a momentary adjustment of my eyes, I see there are hundreds of people milling about and talking in a droning, anxious-sounding, medium high-pitched tone.

I keep my sweats on over my shorts and long sleeve shirt. A voice over a megaphone asks that runners check in. I walk carefully and slowly past and around the masses of moving figures toward the imploring voice. I locate several people, one holding a clipboard, and give them my name and number. Other runners are doing the same.

The half hour before the race is like one big party; I greet old running friends. My crew members and I walk around everywhere, sopping up the energy and enthusiasm, trying to prepare for the start, but seemingly getting nothing accomplished. Warmup isn't really necessary; just a few quick tentative stretches are enough. Going off by myself to get mentally prepared doesn't seem necessary. All these preliminaries I can do after the race begins, on the slow jog-walk atmosphere of the first 4.7 miles to the top of the mountain.

Somewhere friends take some pictures; other friends get lost in the hubbub. This is sure a lot of fun, I think, and it hits me that I will soon try to run 100 miles. Yet there is no time for urgency before the start. The race will begin casually, slowly, and with a lot of celebration, I feel, and then will get even slower as we progress snail-like up the dirt road into the darkness and away from the crowd.

I finally go make a last visit to the restroom; from now on the outdoors will be my bathroom. I shed my sweats, check to make sure my water bottles are full and secured and that I have everything I want in my waist pack. I clip on the belt, adjust my cap, and I'm ready to depart.

As the precious minutes before the start of the race wind down to an isolated few moments, I reach back to my thoughts a couple of weeks ago. I remember seriously asking myself what it is that is so very special about this grueling event that causes me to desire the attempt to conquer its so very awesome distance and course. My soul searches for some reason for the lure of the trails, the mountains, the avenue of the Western States Trail.

I believe each of us is an artist, creative in a unique way. Each one of us expresses that artistic nature through a different medium. Some people use paint brushes on their canvases; others play musical instruments to create unique sounds. Many act out parts on a stage, becoming make believe characters and turning them into believable people; a large group put words into thought-flowing combinations that fascinate readers. Most of us who hit the roads and trails express our artistic talents through our long distance running.

I am a running artist. My paintbrush brandishes vivid images across a canvas of mountain trails. Each rock, every bush brushing my legs, water rushing over huge boulders, dead leaves crinkling under my shoes in the shade of an old tree: this is my background. The main subject of my picture is my running, hours upon hours of padding along with the music of my steps, reaching and grabbing for every little innuendo of the trail.

The goal of my 100 mile race is not to finish it in under 24 hours. The main goal is experiencing the moment of time during the 24 hours or so of the race itself. The athletic event is the goal; 24 hours, more or less, is a moment when everything stands still, when time itself seems suspended in air. The race is my courage, my training, my trust in a higher being, the deep gut loneliness of my soul isolated in nature's wilderness where no one is able to tell me how I should feel and what I should seek. My body and mind will encounter night, day, and night again, the awful, gritty desolation of moving forward against that wall of time and distance, yet forever standing still in the enormity of the task.

Pain cannot be shared with anyone watching or helping me. The rhythmic agony creeps on and on, hour after hour, moving up and down, grabbing for heaven one moment and then dipping into hell the next. Just 24 hours; one soul may never again put so much of life and heaven into one full day. The goal of my 100 mile run is the run itself. From when the gun is fired to the finish line, I view a different world, the canvas on which my artistic expression bares itself, my soul present for the world to see but for no one except me to feel.

I am a hero to myself; my preparation and race are my heroic acts. It can be no other way. I know I am not crazy; others have traveled this path before me and they are sane. I am my own hero. Fright strikes my mind when I think about it; will I be ready for this task, I keep asking myself? I don't know the answer to that overpowering question, but, yes, I am looking forward to finding out the answer, which I will discover one painful way or another in a relatively precious few hours.

I may find myself a spectator looking at myself as I run and walk, observing myself fighting the small and large battles I will surely encounter. Like life, I may win or I may lose these battles; the only thing that really counts is that I will fight the main skirmish on the battlefront itself, meeting the enemy head on, the trails, the heat and cold, the pain and fatigue, the ghosts of the mind, the endless, endless miles. Even if I lose this battle, I have won a personal war for I have challenged. I have challenged and my soul knows this victory too.

The magnitude of the event is awe-inspiring. I can easily pass it off as just another crazy event that I happen to sign up for. Joking about the almost shear stupidity of doing the race is a simple game I can play. Some may believe only a slightly insane person might attempt such an undertaking, yet I honestly can say that I have complete control of my mental faculties. Every time I briefly contemplate on what I am about to partake, a thin, quick shaft of inner fear jolts my mind. Endless unformed questions enter my consciousness with just as many blank answers reflecting back at me.

Yes, I'm looking forward to the challenge; I am looking forward to this meeting with pain. I am anxiously looking forward to painting my picture across the trails. As that spectator I am interested in the outcome, but I am looking forward much more toward putting one foot in front of the other, of being a pioneer, gaining ground, and maybe feeling a little bit of heaven and even experiencing a little bit of hell along the way. I feel a little sorry for those who will never engage this experience. I'm sorry they may never know what they are missing, really missing. In these ultra events I experience much more than the easy life of the non-effort; I experience the heavenly spirit of active life itself.

So many intangibles will determine my fate as I am now about to take my first easy steps on my first Western States Endurance Run. I am now out there with my other comrades in arms, each of us determined to give our very best. We will draft on each other's energy; some of us will fail along the way; that is the inevitable nature of the race itself. Others of us will win our battles. The important thing is not the results; it is that we are putting our souls on the line. With that fact alone, our races shall be won.

We now charge together as one body in the excitement of a sprint, all 415 of us, up the dirt and rocky road and trail to the top of the mountain, 4.7 miles to Emigrant Monument, the top of the Squaw Valley Ski Area. This is 100 miles, not a 10K race, so what is the hurry? The press is to get away from all the pre-race hoopla, the endless meetings, the physicals, the procuring of souvenirs, the introductions of top runners and race personalities, and the looking at cameras and spotlights. The breathless haste is to get on the mountain where we all belong, to be alone only as running beings, to get ourselves settled down and mentally reposed at the beginning of our long journey, 100 miles across the fearful, respected Sierra Nevada mountain range.

We are all companions together, charging as one brigade out after the unseen enemy, all with the desperate dream that aches in the deepest recesses of our hearts. Some are faster than others, but all are after the same objective, the finish line at Auburn. Without having to speak the thought to each other we know that about half of us will fail to reach that finish line, but we all know it will be the other guy not making it. We are like mates out to find the battle front. Some of us will come back; others will never return, learning only that defeat will temporarily shatter that incurable, heroic vision of the silver at the end of the trail.

No one talks about it because we don't want to face the reality that the months of fantasies may be suddenly dashed away by a sudden fall, an imperceptible pain breeding into a monster, an upset stomach subduing one to a driveling idiot begging for release from this appalling hell. No amount of physical conditioning and mental toughness can prepare any of us from some unforseen demon who decides to play games with our bodies and minds.

Of the half who finish, fewer than half of those will probably make it under 24 hours, the deadline to achieve the coveted Silver Belt Buckle, the most sought after prize in the world of ultra endurance running. The buckle, for anyone who possesses one, is a rare symbol of courage, fortitude, and sheer guts.

For awhile we proceed in a group up a dirt service road, trying to hold back any exhaustive effort; passing each other is tight and difficult. Roger and I go together for a few minutes, stumbling together next to the massive, surging group beside us. As the hill steepens, some of us walk while others run by, all of us slowly trying to gauge our speed to avoid quick fatigue. Some of the walkers begin to run slowly, and some of those

The runners charge to the top of Squaw Valley Ski area and Emigrant Gap.

running fall into a walk. Back and forth we stagger up the grade, saying little to each other as we pass and re-pass, light dust stirring the cool, breezy, thin, summer mountain air. Somewhere Roger surges ahead of me for good; I will never see him again during the race.

The morning light slowly and almost imperceptibly begins to penetrate the darkness. A yellow-orange dim glow brightens the eastern sky. Faces and clothes become less blurred as we move slowly upward. Braking to a walk, a large group of us trudge up a steep section, each of us planting one foot slowly in front of the other in rhythm with the walking, unheard music of our group. We move in tune with the others in front and beside us, in turn spreading unseen the motion to those behind us.

The old road levels slightly, one walker picking up his feet and beginning a trot. The next runner follows suit, then another, until all of us except a few saner souls are running now in unison, our steps, our breathing, our bouncing waist belts, our surging thoughts, all advancing as one entity. We aren't consciously sure if this is the correct pace, but everyone is doing it, plus it is too early to feel any fatigue. Onward we all shuffle as one.

Then suddenly in the dim, mounting rising morning light, David and Jeff, two members of our crew, appear in front of me standing beside the trail. They had gone up the trail before the beginning of the race in the pre-dawn darkness for a couple of miles to greet Roger and me. I feel a little warm wearing the long sleeve shirt with which I start the race, despite the fact that the air is still cool and a brisk breeze sweeps across the snow-depleted ski slopes.

However, I know the air will become warmer as I progress, so I risk being chilled for awhile and exchange my long sleeve shirt for a dry short sleeve one. As I put on the shirt, David and Jeff inform me that Roger has gone out fast as usual and is quite a distance ahead of me already. As we exchange quiet small talk other runners climb steadily past me, making me anxious to get going again. I thank them for their help and leave them to resume their downward journey as I continue on upward at a slow trot.

Casually I glance over my right shoulder and look back down toward the valley floor and notice the tremendous distance all of us have gained on vertical. A long, slowly moving line of tiny, red lights wind snakelike across the still dark valley. Another runner looks also and remarks that all the crews and spectators are heading out of the valley; they all appear in such a great hurry. These hundreds of people finally leave us runners alone for awhile, 415 of us now by ourselves and yet united as one, like an army, but these same people will join us later on, hours away, to help us renew our bodies and our spirits. We are alone now as the skies continue to brighten perceptibly, alone on our journey to the top of the mountain.

We leave the comfort of the dirt road for a narrow, rocky trail, climbing upwards through the brush, crossing old fire roads every few minutes. The trail is so narrow, uneven, and cut so deep into the mountain that each of us must walk with our legs close together to avoid scraping the brush hanging over the sides. We primarily walk, climbing in a long single line, one person right after another. When one of us walks, all of us walk. When one tries to run, all of us run. We are too close together to do anything else.

Passing each other is almost impossible because the trail is so narrow and rutty; but this is early in the run, so there is no need to be a hero. We all slow down and enjoy our walk and jog, chattering to each other of things to come and our fears of the mountain, observing the strange scene that surrounds us.

The dark, cool, morning air throws its crisp breeze through our shirts, as we climb higher toward the sky, causing us to shiver slightly in the perspiration released by our exertion. I methodically and carefully place one foot in front of the other, securing each hold solidly before making my next step. I am aware of others ahead of me and behind me doing the same things, with an occasional mistake causing a clattering of rolling rocks and mumbled curses. I sense more than hear the deep breathing of hundreds of lungs. We are like one long snake, each slightly bent forward at the waist, leaning forward to drive ourselves as one force up the mountain.

The early morning twilight begins its brightening of the eastern sky until mere shadows of white-clad runners become vivid images of mechanical-like people moving steadily onward and upward. The sun breaks through about half way up and like a strobe light brightens the upper slopes, glaring brilliance reflecting off the snow bank near the top. The shadow line of the sun and the eastern horizon gives off the stark contrast of the fire-white snow with the black-white snow that hasn't tasted yet the orange glare of the sunny orb.

Looking upward, I see a solid single file of runners hundreds of feet above me, and turning around to look below, I observe others in a seemingly endless line following in our footsteps. Someone nearby in our line chuckles and comments that it looks like an all out attack on the mountains with full army troops. He is absolutely correct; it is an armed assault, but the enemy is something unseeable; it is more than the mountain; inside each of us is our personal commitment to this race. We all know we can help each other and we desire every other runner success, but we also know we each must win our own individual battles and conquests along the way. Some of our new found comrades will win; others will sadly lose the battle. At this time early in the race no one knows who the winners will be, who the survivors will be. We continue on, plodding upwards one step at a time, our eyes focused ahead of our feet.

Slowly we clamor up the last bank of snow to Emigrant Monument, planting each step safely in a foothold in the snow, where the television crew greets us; numerous spectators and race officials also cheer us on.

Some runners release pent-up shouts of joy at reaching the top, the wind blowing their yells into the crackling, fresh air. Other runners pause for a moment to look at the view of Lake Tahoe in front of the rising sunlight. Others take on a little refreshment before continuing down the other side. I decide to stop, look backward for the last time and suck in a final breath of the cool, flag-snapping, summer breeze, my skin chilling slightly under my short sleeve shirt at this 9,000 feet elevation point.

I walk over behind a boulder and urinate one more time before continuing downward. My reward of a minute or two respite here on the highest spot of the course will pay dividends much later on during the day and night. The breeze is crisp and strong on top of the mountain. I take in one final glance of the tremendous vista of mountains and canyons that await me. There is a subconscious warning in the air, telling us that we can enjoy the stop but had better not linger for very long if we want to find the finish line over 95 miles away. This climb has only been the warmup; once off the other side it is time for business to begin in quiet, determined earnest.

The hoopla is gone; the beginning is behind us; the rocky path is ahead of us. Each of us must now reach down and begin the real journey ahead, the physical and mental torture that we all know we must endure together, yet overcome individually. The first tiny steps of the Western States 100 Mile Endurance Run are over, and many more giant steps wait for us during the next 24 hours. The mountains and canyons, the cold, the biting wind, the oppressive, windless heat, the tall trees, the dust, snow, rocks, streams, and mud all reach their hands out at once and tell us to come on if we dare to tread forth to challenge their domain. There is no turning back now. We will either succeed or fail for heaven to see; there cannot be a middle ground. Our souls are open for all others watching on the trail to observe; we shall succeed or perish before the eyes of the world. But we will try very hard. Oh, will we try!

Seven and a half years prior to starting this race I am reborn, for on the fateful day of January 1, 1979, I became a runner. Not that my life before that date was by any means unsuccessful or not fulfilled. Life was going fairly smoothly, with an ongoing teaching and coaching career that was keeping me busy all the time. All through my life I had been involved in a variety of sports, both team and individual, and I enjoyed immensely the great outdoors.

However, in my busy life I had put on just a little too much weight and was beginning to feel I was just a bit too unhealthy to continue this lifestyle successfully. On that special day, the first day of the year, I made an seemingly innocent resolution, one that I would faithfully keep and expand upon for the rest of my life leading up to the present day some 28 years later.

My resolution is that I will run an average of two miles a day for the entire year of 1979. Although I am somewhat overweight, I am still in fairly decent physical shape, and I somehow fancy myself as an above average athlete. My favorite outdoor sports and activities include snow skiing, tennis, softball, fishing, and backpacking, and I am fairly proficient at all of them. Looking back at pictures of me at that time, I see that I am way too much overweight, terribly unequipped with any degree of skill to handle anything decently physical in nature.

Over a year later I learn that ordinary people can actually race, and it's a total of a year and a half before I jump into my first race, a four miler. A group of us decide to run the race; I wear a pair of worn out sneakers. I still haven't purchased a pair of running shoes. I have no running T-shirts; I feel out of place at the starting line. I find tremendous physical and emotional satisfaction finishing the race and being able to test myself against the distance of the course and my own ability. Although every race after that is still a painful experience, I keep doing more of them and anticipate each new race with a kind of almost sadistic pleasure.

I become a dedicated runner from this slow beginning, and I believe the year and a half of jogging before doing my first race builds up my mileage base, my patience to do things correctly, and my desire to work hard to achieve my goals in running. I am now on my way.

CHAPTER 3
WARMING UP AT RED STAR RIDGE
(16.5 MILES)

Far away there in the sunshine are my
highest aspirations. I may not reach them,
but I can look up and see their beauty,
believe in them, and try to follow where they lead.
(Saying)

I top the pass, the sharp morning breeze snapping at my skin, billowing my shirt as I shuffle downward. I take one quick glance at the endless mountain spread out beyond and below my gaze, only a small portion of the terrain that I must try to cross to reach my destination. The noise of the beginning is gone, and I am off and down the other side into oblivion; all of us are now individually on our own for awhile, yet together, as the race has not yet spread out enough to allow for any solitary running.

My memory drifts wistfully back to three weeks previously when a group of us take a training run over this section of trail and encounter the precarious, white vastness of huge, melting snow banks obliterating the markings of the trail. Now just three short weeks later, the warming sun has done its job quite well, relieving us of almost all of the huge white banks, replacing them with melting streams and fresh green grasses and plants.

Suddenly I become that snow runner again, gently negotiating every wrinkle of the uneven trail. Glaring sun stabs at my eyes after bouncing off the pure whiteness of the pockmarked, dirty, melting snow. Long dead, tiny limbs of pine trees lie across the warming iciness of white. Patches of brown and black ground open up between the white humps, clean melt water flowing gently over the oozing mud.

I am a slow runner and pause momentarily before my muddy cleated, shoe bottoms step on the white patch of snowy domain before me. My shoe hits and pushes off, slightly slipping and spinning as I lurch to maintain balance. Gingerly bounding in short strides, I inch forward like a tight rope walker, speed suddenly secondary to avoiding a disastrous slip and fall to the wet, cutting whiteness.

Once my balance is established, I become more bold, slowly increasing my tempo, step after step accelerating to a jog. I reach for the brink of maximum forward speed, yet at the same time cuddling next to the cliff of disaster, the big slip which would leave my body sprawled across the vast, pallid pile of packed snow, my soul temporarily stunned before picking itself up and continuing on.

The sun intensifies its wicked brightness, bouncing off the snow and magnifying its terror. The rays' warmth and subtle burning power jab strongly and directly back at me. The bare skin of my legs accepts the burning like so many other hours and days of sun acceptance before this time.

Sun glasses perch on my nose, the dark lenses obscuring the darting, scanning nervousness of the eyes picking out the next safe foothold. A white cap perches on my head, bouncing back the powerful rays with a soft, cotton glare. My arms barely pump, but instead flare outward in a balancing motion, elbows outside the hands, the fingers curled lightly. My hands and arms move slowly, darting here and there as each new, fresh step plants itself, helping to balance my upper body.

It's a slow careful time for me, this becoming a snow runner. Time speeds up and flies past, but the distance drags behind. The urge to speed up temporarily takes over as I encounter a level smooth patch. My legs glide easily but tensely over the white pond, each step daring to move a fraction of a second faster than the last one. The mood holds only a moment as I slip, my shoe flailing out in an awkward sideways movement, the tendons of my knee and lower leg tightening and bracing to counter the shock and keep the balance.

I am a snow runner, on top of the world, among the conifers and pines searching for some answer to the question of the mountain. When it is over, the shoes are wet and muddy, the socks soaked, the skin a little more red, the breath a little quicker, the muscles more tired with aches in new places never felt before. The mileage is low and the speed slow; there is no flow to the running. The eyes squint with sun tears and the agony of painful white lightning. I am a member of an exclusive club; I am a snow runner.

Coming back to the present I see that all the snow from that run is gone, but I face another urgent problem, wet and muddy surfaces from the runoff. My legs feel loose and relaxed as I try to establish a comfortable downhill pace along the first ridge. The trail dodges in and out of bushes and trees, over some rocks, across a log, and on top of an occasional remnant of a snow bank still trying to survive in the summer heat but slowly bleeding icy water and losing the battle in the warming air.

I climb briefly several times, slowing down once to negotiate a narrow section over some mud and a flowing stream cascading down a narrow chute between two patches of high brush. This early in the race runners go in packs from four up to ten or so, with individual members occasionally breaking away. Passing one another is possible but done very carefully; the runner behind must notify the runner in front what his intentions are. The lead runner often senses that the following runner is gaining ground and will ask if he wants to pass before the trailing runner actually makes the request.

I find myself held back by the group of runners I am with, so I pass them and establish some distance between us. I nearly reach another group ahead of me when I must stop to urinate. By the time I finish my chore a couple members of my former group pass me, and I must catch up and pass them again. This leapfrog effect happens several times. It is obviously irritating to stop every 15 or 20 minutes to drain myself of fluids, but it is a good sign that I am hydrating well. The logistics of running with and past other runners this early in the venture is a real challenge, but does help me stay patient, which may aid later on in the day by not making me tired now.

I now encounter the wetness of the trail over and over again; somehow I feel the trail is trying to hold me back in my pursuit. The water softly splashes over the rocks and trickles across my running domain, my trail, softly winding its way through the rocks, the wild mountain flowers and plants. It drops slowly but steadily at crazy angles as it pulls dirt loose from the trail, creating a myriad of tiny gullies.

I slow appreciably as I approach the stream that joins my trail. I rivet my eyes toward every possible dry spot as I jump awkwardly and bowlegged from one dry rock to another. Before taking one particular step my eyes dart everywhere but cannot find a dry spot. Lightly I step toward a shallow, muddy spot, hoping I don't sink in. I place my foot and quickly lift my weight and jump with the opposite foot all in one motion to land on a small root from a nearby bush. I am not quick enough as the weight on my first shoe pushes it half way down into the mud, water and goo oozing up the side as I jerk it quickly up, sucking to pull loose and be free. I quickly hop off my now dry foot, seeking another solid support with my half-wet shoe.

Finding a solid rooty mass of water-soaked lichen, my shoe seeks its support. My eyes dart ahead in the same moment, seeking support for my still dry shoe. I see only shallow, flowing water seeping down along the half-rocky, half-wet, dirt trail. I push off the roots and leap ahead, my arms spread out chimp fashion to keep a delicate balance. In an instant, I make an instinctive, midair decision, and awkwardly seek out the only solid looking goo available that might hold my weight.

I guess correctly this time but cannot celebrate as I'm already deciding my next foot plant and am eye-darting ahead for fractions of a second for future landing spots. I see three, four steps ahead, and decide two or three steps ahead. Sometimes I have no choice and simply must plop in the wet and sometimes dirt-water mixture and get out as fast as possible.

Moving ahead like an awkward, tightrope walker, probably going too quickly, I feel moisture seeping against my skin from the wet socks. I mentally block the discomfort as a normal penalty for making steady, forward progress, first one step, gradually bunches of yards, and slowly mile upon mile.

I run the wet as a skillful technician, with no time to think of overall progress. I am zeroed to my task, reaching for that next leap, aware of a focused clarity of the nuances of the constantly changing features of the trail. Each step, each fine combination of rock, stick, dirt, and water is unique; never is the trail the same in two spots. I run like a paint brush across a unique canvas, each stroke different but important to the whole picture of making it to a desired unified completion.

The trail temporarily smooths out and running is made easy again, but soon the hope that such running will remain is shattered by the seed of knowledge that the long winter snow runoff must in some way continue to find its way to the streams and canyons below. The snow melt must continue on its crazy route down the uneven mountainside, carving its own paths to complete the journey. The water, like myself, has a voyage to complete. We must compete on the same trail, but we respect each other as we cross paths on our treks to our individual destinations.

I hear the slosh of running water ahead. This time I see thick, brush lush from winter growth powering its tentacles across the flowing water, often the branches touching each other from opposite sides of the creek. This time I see a full born stream, rushing over rocks and gurgling in the quiet eddies. I hop up the stream, from rock to rock, this time with many solid footholds from which to pick. The water trickles narrowly past my shoes, continuing its downward trip to some remote canyon, playing with the mountainside during its descent.

I slow down with the steepness of the slope, pushing a branch away from the path with my arm. One step is short; the next stretches to reach a solid, more distant foothold. Finally the trail levels out and I secure better footing for several yards and relax my next half a dozen strides.

Now a stream crosses the trail at a perpendicular angle and I encounter mud during the last few feet. I jump again, trying to locate the solid part but am only partially successful, as my foot sinks in. The new mud seeps quickly over the old, caked on, and partially dry mud already formed up the sides of my shoes. I pull out quickly once again and hop to the next dry spot.

The trail meanders on in this fashion for several miles, broken only by periodic deviations of dry sections, the small sections that give the legs and the mind a brief moment of relief. Then it is back to the wet again, the rocks, the mud, the brush.

I meld to the elements of the wet trail. I must tame them enough to win my race. I cannot conquer these elements, so I must work with and not fight against them. I brake to slow down and analyze each new section which is completely unlike anything that comes before or follows after it. The various sections of trail may look the same, but never are the elements the same size or made up in the same combination as the previous section of wet trail.

Patience is my password; caution is my code word of attack. I will make it through safely; my shoes, socks, and feet may be wet and muddy, my muscles may find new aches, and my concentration may be extended to its limit, but I make it past all the wet challenges to the dryness of the trail beyond. I am a runner of water and mud. It is part of my experience, and I know I can run it because I must do so to succeed. I run and I succeed; I am a runner of the ground elements and nothing can deny me my success.

I glance upward toward the sky and notice the sun having trouble pushing out from behind a cloud bank, which is good news because the air remains cool. The wind has subsided to a breeze by now, but it still has a moderately, nippy effect on my skin. As I glide easily across the side of the ridge, the trail suddenly begins to drop dramatically. I am running on an old fire road now. The footing is fairly solid, but I still keep my eyes glued to the surface to avoid any unseen rocks that might trip me and cause a spill. Down and down I go and I soon hear voices; Hodgson's Cabin, just under ten miles into the course.

This is a miner's cabin, and as I drop straight down the slope at a braking skid, I see a group of other runners filling their bottles from a well behind the cabin and from a couple of aid personnel dishing it out from a giant can. I call out my number to a person standing by the trail with a clipboard, walk over to the can and fill my bottles, and quickly head out. I notice a crowd of runners filling their own bottles. A few moments ago I was running virtually alone, but after the aid station the trail suddenly seems congested again. I stop to find a bush to urinate for what must be about the tenth time. Three other runners pass quickly by me; I know my hydration is good and my weight must be up, although I have no sure way of knowing for several hours yet.

I continue running steadily downhill briefly and then settle into an even pace along the top of a ridge that rolls with the trail like a carnival ride. My legs exude strength and power, and my stomach is calm. The trail goes up and down; I walk when it gets a little steep, move comfortably when it is level, and step out lively when it darts downhill. There are open areas, areas of tall trees, with occasional sections of rocks and brush. All I want to do now is compose myself and establish my pace, stay relaxed, and reach the next station, Red Star Ridge, the first really major stopping point.

I start up the ridge with one of the race's major landmarks ahead of me, Cougar Rock, a steep barren rock high on the ridge. It comes at just over 12 miles, and this is where the photographers line up to snap pictures of the runners. It is here that many of the most famous shots of the Western States are displayed in newspapers and magazines. Pictures taken here bring out the ruggedness of the trail and the breathtaking beauty and grandeur of the mountains and canyons in the background. Next to the trail the mountainside drops sharply downward into a green, forested canyon. Peaks from eight miles back can be seen as distant majestic vistas.

Sure enough two photographers are snapping pictures as we approach. I am in a large group running single file, about ten of us staying in pace as one and finding mental strength from each other. As we cross the rocks, a runner two places ahead of me suddenly trips and sprawls without warning across the rocks, skidding and breaking the fall with his hands. The next runner and I stop to check him out as he picks himself up. He says he is okay except for a couple of bruises; it is amazing that he can still run. I continue following the others in a walk up the short section past Cougar Rock, glancing at the photographers snapping pictures.

Cougar Rock at just over 12 miles into the race.

We pass Cougar Rock and continue on. The trail now becomes dusty; in places the red-brown powder comes up over our ankles. The pathway snakes down a narrow gully, where earlier melt water has eroded and carved out a narrow funnel. Short pine and fir trees closely line the trail, branches reaching out to touch us. Awkwardly jamming my shoes against the bank I hop from side to side, avoiding the gully, then finally stumble right down the middle of the chute. Picking the best footing is difficult. Worse, we still run in single file, and the trailing runners are choked by the flying cloud of dust created by the preceding runners.

It looks like a dust storm. The footing is soft in the dust, and my shoe slides with each step like being on ice until the shoe cleats find some hard pack or a root or rock to bite into, gripping like a clamp. I shift all my weight on to the biting shoes, feeling the support grabbing through my soles and ankles, and push off to the next step. I fly downhill, half coasting and out of control, seeking the next solid spot with each foot plant, again sliding and gripping and pushing off.

With each step a puff of brown dust scrapes off with friction between shoes and dirt and drifts up to my face; the dust fights with my eyes to blur my vision, settling on my face, arms, legs, and clothing. Step after step, puff after puff of dust; layers as thin as microfilm pile upon me, slowly changing my cleanliness into part of the dust trail, a part of the wilderness. I become part of the trail itself.

I hear some laughter and a couple of expletives coming from behind me, the voices echoing off the trees of the gradually deepening shadows of the woods. I too curse softly to myself, but inside I laugh a small chuckle as I realize how silly we must all look. This an open invitation to an accident, I think. But I continue on; it is only part of the race, a part of the contract we must all fulfill to reach the finish. I must try just to concentrate a little bit more precisely on each step until I can escape from this group of fellow runners.

Down a steep hill we rush; now I hear chattering, enthusiastic voices. People appear ahead, and I know I am approaching the first major organized aid station, Red Star Ridge. Suddenly in an opening on a small flat spot in the deep woods the station appears. I check in; people offer to fill my bottles as I rip them hurriedly off my pack. A table has all kinds of food; it looks like the goodies offered at someone's party. I grab a banana and a couple of salty crackers and stuff them into my mouth. Some crew members of others runners shout encouragement while they are waiting for their runners. My crew will greet me for the first time later on at Robinson Flat. Other runners like myself mill around the tables, savoring the cuisine, not sure whether to stay or push on, the temptation of the food trying to tug on them not to leave this paradise.

My bottles are refilled and I am ready to leave, something always difficult to do because I would like to be able to relate to all these people what the race is really like out there. Already I feel like I have run a full race, and I want them to know how tough it is. Inside my head I know I have really just begun my journey; so far I have run only the warmup. I secure a bottle in my left hand and take off for Duncan Canyon. I have now completed over 16 miles of the race.

As I continue my racing, seeds are slowly planted to do the further distances, first the half marathon in the winter of 1981, my first marathon in the summer of 1981, and my first 50 miler in 1984. The long races I seem to enjoy much more than the short ones, perhaps because I can rely on my best asset, endurance, and not have to always be frustrated with my lack of natural speed. I look forward to testing myself further and further, to see just how far I can go, and the further I go, the further I know I could have gone. My racing becomes a test of myself against my physical conditioning and exertion. Slowly it becomes something more, a sort of ritual and expression of self that I must enact to continually prove myself to me, to become a hero to myself.

I'm not a fast racer, logging only a modest 3:06 personal best in the marathon, and I usually have to work hard to get into the 38 or 39 range for the 10 kilometer race. In fact, it takes me several years to break 40 minutes. However, I find I seem to have an inherited ability to go for long periods of time non-stop at a slow, steady pace. Some of my friends call me Clydesdale, in reference to the big horses who just seem to plod along forever, strong horses who don't proceed very rapidly but can trot on for long periods of time and demonstrate abundant strength.

Sometime during a mountain marathon I run with Bob, and that is the first time I hear about the Western States Endurance Run. At that time I have no desire to try it, but the distance and the silver buckle award intrigue me greatly. Later I do my first 50 miler, and I meet and talk to people who have done this crazy 100 miler across the Sierras. The planted seed is now nurtured and starts to receive further consideration.

I begin to really wonder. Is it actually possible that a person of ordinary ability like myself could actually complete one of these insane-sounding races?

CHAPTER 4
ROBINSON FLAT - FIRST CREW ACCESS
(30.2 MILES)

The woods are lovely, dark and deep.
But I have promises to keep,
And miles to go before I sleep,
And miles to go before I sleep.
                                        (Robert Frost)

Red Star Ridge to the Duncan Canyon station is about eight miles with another six miles to Robinson Flat, and I glide evenly along the rolling trail as it traverses up and down along the top edge of a narrow ridge, the sides falling off sharply in some locations. My body is now well along into the race, and my legs exude power and warmth. With a steady even trail, they feel relaxed and comfortable with each stride. The dust continues to drift up into my nostrils and cover my clothes and skin when I slide and stumble down a steep section, but the runners are spreading out on the course now, and the clouds of dust have diminished to small puffs that accompany each individual runner, quickly dispersing into the cool, morning air.

I am aware of the brutal condition of my shoes, the reddish-brown dust sticking in layers on to the previous moisture from the snow melt higher on the mountain. My once beautiful dark blue shoes look like they belong to the junk heap. My socks are also damp, and I can sense the wetness along the skin of my feet. The moisture isn't a problem yet as I haven't felt the beginning of blisters forming, that familiar slowly creeping, very fine local pain. The longer I continue running the more my feet dry out. I know that I will have relief at Robinson Flat at 30 miles when my crew gives me dry shoes and socks.

The trail suddenly gets very steep uphill for a short section, and I walk to recuperate. Methodically I step, my knees bent; I put my weight on my foot, straighten out my leg, and push off up the hill. Over and over I repeat the movement, my head down observing the terrain. I don't dare look up because the top will look too far away and may depress me mentally. I try to disassociate my mind from the task. Soon the trail begins to level out. I begin to be aware of the light, very white, cloud cover encasing the mountains, very thin, high altitude clouds that are harmless but cool me off by preventing the rays of the sun from penetrating my skin. The temperature is still very pleasing, but I remember the training run over this segment several weeks ago when our group encountered a wet, brief thunderstorm. I certainly don't need something like that today.

I begin picking up my feet faster now and soon am running at a slow jog again, my feet barely sliding across the surface of the dirt and rocks. As the trail starts curving downhill, I turn over my legs faster, until I am running at a pace when a moment of lax concentration can cause a damaging fall. Many miles of practicing this walking and running in unison let me avoid the stiffness some runners may feel every time they start up running. There are times when I wonder whether my legs will actually run after I've been walking for a long period of time. There is an inner fear that my legs won't be able to start up, but somehow they always do. My constant practice of this start and stop exercise makes it easy to handle mentally as well as physically during the race.

I check my watch and know that I should be getting close to the next aid station. Off to my left I glance way down the mountainside several thousand feet into the canyon and see a landmark, French Meadows Reservoir, a sign that Duncan Canyon is not far away. I remember this landmark from my training run when a veteran runner told me at this point that we were almost there. It is one of the few brief moments so far that I have even looked at the scenery. It is a vast sight, one of remoteness, a sign of handiwork designed carefully and molded by some higher being than the human race.

I stop momentarily on an uphill segment and look back, beholding the noble pinnacles and crests of mountains I have come across, many miles behind me, the distance seemingly vast, endless, and truly imposing. I suddenly feel very small and ant-like atop this great vista, a small speck lost along the tiny footpath, amidst giant firs and pines and beside the crackling of wild, never ending, fast flowing cold water streams. As if to give an exclamation mark to my thoughts, the breeze suddenly picks up and the clouds shift to let the sun poke its rays around the white edges of the bloated puffiness.

I race down the hill at just under breakneck velocity, only a short distance now from the checkpoint. Abruptly I hear the yelling and shouting of voices echoing through the forest somewhere down near the bottom of the hill, indicating that I am close. Still several minutes pass before I arrive at this outrageously joyous welcoming party. Ahead are small flags several feet apart lining the chute to the aid station. A friendly person on the trail tells me to go left, that I'll be coming back his way again, and to watch for other runners. I feel like I'm entering the pit stop area of a major raceway.

Because of the logistics of getting their supplies in, the station personnel design the approach to this station as a circle where the runners leave on the same trail they enter and see other runners going the opposite direction. The flags line the entire circle and people cheer near the tables of food and drink. It seems confusing and almost like a carnival ride, but all I can do is take it in stride. Several people offer me help at once as I skid to a sudden stop; someone fills my bottles; I grab at some of the numerous items of food that are available. I munch at the food, trying to wash it down with water, talking lightly and quietly to the personnel who are there.

Everyone seems almost too happy and too friendly, trying to please runners in every way. I wonder how there can be so many joyous people so far out in this lonely wilderness area. Obviously they are well rested and fresh too just like the runners who are still in the early stage of the race. Will the people who man the stations 60 miles on down the trail be just as giving of themselves and just as enthusiastic? People I don't know call out my name and wish me luck. As I gather fresh food and supplies, I hear the applause and cheers for another runner coming in behind me.

I grab a handful of pretzels, receive my bottles back full of water, and start out the opposite way, passing a runner coming into the checkpoint. The same person I met entering the station is standing on the trail, this time reminding me to continue on the main pathway. I hear voices echoing in the trees on the bank above me as others are coming into the station. I walk for a couple of minutes, still munching on my food, trying to swallow it too quickly, washing it down with water, realizing that at this point, I don't need to be in a tremendous hurry. I need to take a little time to make sure my nourishment is complete. The surge of adrenalin has caused me to rush through the aid station; I need to ease back down to an even keel again before I go back to my grinding routine on the trail.

Another runner jogs slowly up behind me and passes me while I stop for a moment to rinse down my last bite. I say something unintelligibly to him about finishing lunch before going on. I intend to be humorous but he seems to be in his own world and ignores me. I pick up my feet and take out in pursuit of him. I catch up quickly, latch on to him for a moment, and then pass him again, leaving him far behind. I am now on my way to Robinson Flat, the first medical checkpoint just six miles away.

As I embark to Robinson Flat, my legs feel renewed from the enthusiastic welcome and rest at the last stop. A calmness, a relaxed attitude envelops both my mind and body, an almost numb feeling of self-induced hypnosis. The trail sweeps in a rolling fashion through an enchanted, wooded area. For a while the path has sections of up and down, which seem to go on endlessly before the trail finally levels off and starts flowing tamely downhill toward Duncan Creek.

This is a splendid time and place to run, the dark, green shadows from the lofty trees and thick, tall vegetation casting themselves as canopies over the pathway. The trail is relatively smooth, often covered with pine needles and other forest debris. My legs begin to turn over faster and faster, flowing effortlessly down the narrow path, around quick corners, hopping occasional rocks and dead sticks that have tumbled from the trees. Abruptly no other runners are in front or behind me, and for a few minutes at least I can enjoy the solitude that I have been seeking for the last 24 miles. Being by myself precipitates an inner feeling of a dream-like, non-racing environment, one in which I am alone in the woods with no one aware that I am here.

Things are going so well that my mind begins to wander a little, which means disaster if my concentration fails to detect just one seemingly insignificant obstacle in the trail. Almost trance-like I drift down the trail little aware that near disaster is about to strike, and that before the six miles is over I will battle through one of my most difficult stretches of the race.

I suddenly snake awake as my left shoe hangs up on a small rock on the trail and I plunge forward in midair, my body parallel to the ground. I experience my first and only fall of the race, but just before I land, I throw out my hands quickly, palms down, to keep the force of the impact off my legs, my most valuable possession. Fortunately pine needles cover the trail and the only thing I hurt is my pride. I skid a little on the duff covered trail, balancing on my hands and feet, spread-eagled face down.

I alight slightly on the lower side looking toward the trail. I clamber up slowly to my feet and inspect my body. My hands are just dirty with no cuts, and a little smudge of dirt covers part of one knee where it slightly touched the trail. I curse my stupidity out loud, but no one sees or hears me. I shake with a tiny chuckle at how ridiculous I must look. Now my mind rivets back on the course, no longer mesmerized in a trance-like state. It's back to work.

I pick up the steady, musical tune of a stream gurgling ahead. I observe softly flowing water as it trips downward over small stones, settling momentarily in a quiet pool. I cross Duncan Creek very carefully not wanting to fall down again. The creek is fairly wide, but there are rocks and small boulders spread throughout the bed for foot plants. I can tell some stones are slippery from the water still perched on them left by previous runners splashing through the stream. I hop from rock to rock gingerly and finally make it across; I set out up the fairly long and medium-pitched ascent out of the green canyon.

I hear a loud noise and look back about 50 yards just as another runner falls face first into the creek, having slipped on a rock. He appears to be all right as I hear a couple of loud, angry expletives. He scrambles to his feet while another runner waits for him on the other side of the creek, so I continue my trek upwards. Soon I move toward a runner perched on a rock bent over in obvious discomfort. He has a bad moment which will pass, he tells me in a calm, alert voice. Don't I know about bad moments! I would like to discuss the situation with him and comfort him, but my own deadline to Robinson Flat beckons.

This upward slope really isn't as bad as it seems. It is gently steep; the weather is cool with a cloud cover and a nice breeze, and moments ago my legs were renewed with overflowing energy. Suddenly, though, my thighs resist as I trudge sluggishly up the shaded trail. The effort to walk up is labored; what has happened to all my uphill walking training? My entire body hurts now as I slow slightly to regain my strength.

I continue to tromp unrhythmically up the endless switchbacks at a turtle-like pace as a defeated warrior in battle, leaning forward to help drive myself onward; I command myself to make Robinson Flat. My legs yell violently that they don't wish to continue. I experience my lowest point in the race so far, and I'm only about one third of the way into it. I can't believe I can last the full 100 miles, but I have had stretches in 50 milers and have fought my way through them. Previous such encounters allay my fears somewhat. Time flies by as I encounter switchback after switchback, constantly gaining altitude. I can almost sense the quick movement of the sun; it seems to take forever to reach the top of the hill.

Other runners now approach behind me very quickly, appearing in a sudden moment when minutes ago there were none. Several of them pass me, including an energetic woman who blows by me while moving at a very quick walking pace. I will pass her back about ten miles down the trail. Another young male runner blazes past me on the dead run as the trail levels off and I begin to jog again. As the trail levels, I begin relaxing a little, trying to regain my composure. Distant voices and wood sounds echo and vibrate among the tall, large evergreens growing close together in a grassy, green meadow.

People appear on the trail now and tell me that Robinson Flat is just ahead, the first major medical checkpoint on the course. Here my weight will be taken, and I hope I don't weigh below up to only three percent of my starting weight. With all the effort I have used during the last two miles to struggle up the hill, I fear my weight surely will be down. I hope to be right on my starting weight this early in the race. It will be a good sign for my ability to make weight later on in the race.

If my weight is down, even within acceptable limits, I may have more serious problems at other stations. I've been drinking constantly, but swig down quickly what remains in my bottles even though I'm not thirsty as I approach the station. I pick up my feet and run through the funnel of ribbons and people who line the entrance to the station. Hundreds of people are present, which pumps up my adrenaline and renews my energy. I forget temporarily the past several miles; I have difficulty recognizing where the actual checkpoint is.

Standing in the middle of the pathway I recognize Len, a member of my crew, who takes off ahead of me without saying anything, leading me to the scales. One of the race directors, Norm Klein, is present and enthusiastically tells me I am doing well. His words seem strange after my recent bad spell. The medical people take my waist belt and I step on the scales; it registers 173 pounds, one pound over my starting weight of 172. I am surprised but grateful, and giving the situation a second thought,

I become silently elated; my weight appears to not be a problem so far.

I definitely feel exhilarated again as my crew leads me to a lawn chair to tend to my needs. They are enthusiastic and energetic as they change my wet and dirty shoes and socks for dry ones. They give me some extra nourishment, fill two of my plastic bottles with Max, my special drink, and the other one with water, and massage my legs and shoulders. My shoes are soaked with water and mud that will never come out, and my feet are so drenched I need a towel to dry them off. I complain about the last climb really being a bear, but not so loud as to arouse them to any deep concern over my ability to continue.

I attempt to savor my five minute break from all this agony, but no longer than that. I allow my body to droop and totally relax and chat with my friends, but time seems to go by much too fast. I can hear the ticking in my mind speeding up and going out of control like a raging fire. Temptation tugs at me to stay here forever and forget the trail, to call the whole thing off, but I have 70 miles I must complete before my task is finished. My friends ask me so many questions at once about my needs and condition that the whole setup almost seems humorous. I can barely answer them; some questions I really haven't thought about. I make some comments about the difficulty of the trail. They take off my sweat-drenched shirt and put on a dry one.

More than anything else I relish the mental release of seeing familiar faces and hearing familiar, friendly voices of encouragement. For a few short moments civilization occupies my mental presence before I must go back out there alone again, only myself and my soul. They tell me I look great and that I am about an hour ahead of the 24 hour pace, a fact I am already aware of. I really can't feel strongly enough about this bunch of great guys who have sacrificed a lot of their valuable time just for me.

For every successful and even unsuccessful Western States run, a competent crew lurks somewhere behind the runner providing aid, comfort, and a hearty laugh. Most of all my crew must tell me that I look good even if I feel and appear terrible. All runners know that a crew is important, but what does the crew really do during the race, what kind of personalities should the members have individually, and what should the personality of the crew be collectively?

Someone once said that the initials CREW stand for "Cranky Runner, Endless Waiting," so whatever a crew member does, life is often boring for long stretches and the glamour appears and stays for only a few, short minutes. It takes a special type of person who is willing to stay up for 24 hours or more, drive on dusty roads, wait for hours for me to show up and get to actually see and talk with me only a half dozen times during the entire race, an average of once every four hours.

My group of friends is like a pit crew, and I feel like an automobile making a pit stop, having my tires changed, my oil checked, and fuel added to my tank. My windshield is shined and I am sent off down the trail for another few hours of running before meeting my crew again. They change shoes and socks for me, give me a massage, and feed me whatever food and drink I request. They take off my sweaty shirt and put on a dry one; they tell me my pace in relation to the 24 hour deadline. Most of all they give me encouragement and positive feedback. When I am ready to leave, I hate to depart, not because I am tired, but because I will miss their constant bantering and joking.

My crew is a dedicated team; they work together. They aren't required to come and perform these duties. There is no glory or pay for their work. They can earn no buckle for what they do. None of them have run the trail, but they try so hard to understand what it is like, and they try so hard to be understanding. They don't really know what I go through, but they seem genuinely interested enough to want to inwardly know what I encounter out there alone on the trail.

What do they do while they are waiting? Maybe the beer drinkers pass the time with a brew or two. They watch other runners and crews. They meet other crews whose runners are near to me in the race. They talk about the same endless subjects an endless number of times. They maybe worry if I'm going to make the next checkpoint at near the time I'm supposed to, or will I become a casualty like so many other runners? They worry if they will have everything on hand that I may need when I arrive at the next checkpoint.

We are all together for two days and nights before the race at the race site. They attend the meetings and try to get a feel for what is going on, getting information they will need. They fix the meals for the group, leaving me to take a nap or do anything I want during those few moments of spare time we have. They get a little more sleep the last night than I do. They keep telling me that I can do it, not ever sure what it is I really have to do. On the morning of the race they appear more nervous than I am. From wake up time on race morning until the start, I feel unusual calm inside, but I can feel the tension in my crew. Somehow now my mind has left my body and is floating and suspended above me. I'm in neutral, ready to go; my crew seems a little tense.

My crew members are my brothers and helpers during the race. Without them I don't think I can do it, but I know they can't run the race for me. What a helpless feeling it is to be on a crew waiting for me, not knowing whether I may be injured or sick out there by myself and unable to do anything about it. I feel I must succeed for my crew's sake if not for myself. They have put so much time and effort into my race that I can't let them down now. I must exert all energy to arrive at the next station feeling good, at least appearing to be fine so my crew will feel happy.

One of my crew members does understand. He finished under 24 hours last year when I paced him. Does he try to convey to the others what is going on, or does he know that it is useless and keep his thoughts to himself? David is quiet, but he really does know how badly I want that buckle after seeing him get his last year. He knows that I will do everything possible to be there at the next aid station. He knows I will be there.

The ultimate reward for my crew is the finish line if I make it on time. They can share in my victory, as well as they should. My joy is their joy.

Crew chief Richard Rodriguez greets the author at Robinson Flat.

I'm sure my failure will be their failure also. If a smile is on my face, smiles will be on their faces too. I can thank all of them for what they have done, but I really can't put it all in words. I'm sure they know how I feel about them, for they are a part of me. No words can really give out my feelings, because our bond has been beyond words.

To my crew you are all beyond belief. If one of you ever decides to do this race, I will happily volunteer to be part of your crew. Thanks to you Richard Rodriguez, Paul Jaramillo, Len Hansen, Bob Kearney, and David Calderon.

We have an agreement that I will never stay more than five minutes at any one pit stop, and one of my crew members who has been timing my stop says that the five minutes are over. They lift me out of my chair on wobbly legs, chattering all at once, and some other people cheer as I put on my pack; perhaps they are cheering another runner, their own runner. I thank everyone and begin a slow jog to the exit of the aid station looking back and giving one last quick wave. My first major hurdle is over, and I'm off into the warming late morning sunlight and eventually to the two biggest and most difficult canyons on the course. I'm feeling well now, but my race has only begun.

During the fall of 1984 a friend and I send off for applications to the 1985 Western States Run. The application itself is frightening because it asks for so much information, but I fill it out and send it in with my entry fee, wondering if I have done the right thing with the experience of completing only one ultramarathon. I don't get picked that first year, but my friend does. My shock of disappointment gradually gives way to thankfulness as I realize that I can't possibly get ready with so little experience at longer distances and trail running. My friend asks me if I will be his pacer for the race, which means I will accompany him during the final 38 miles of the race, most of it at night; he also has almost no experience at the ultrarunning distances.

My friend David Calderon is an excellent runner, having a sub-2:40 marathon to his credit, but this 100 miler is as new to him as it is to me. He has only run a couple of ultraruns before taking on this new demanding distance. As I join him at Foresthill that Saturday evening and head to the Rucky Chucky River Crossing, I begin a journey of hope and encouragement for him as well as myself.

As a pacer I am responsible for my runner's safety. I try to tend to his needs when he has a problem, and I volunteer moral support along the way. But most of all I discover just how tough this race is on the body and the mind. Here I am rested and fresh joining a friend who has already traveled over 60 miles. I can discern all his weaknesses, his strengths, and his valor and spirit as he forges ahead.

I cannot really comprehend what he is enduring, even though I can sense it by what he reveals to me from what he says and by his body movements. As we pad through the dark with our flashlights trained on the narrow trail ahead of us, I can discern it is deep gut courage that keeps him advancing. I find out that being depleted of energy is no excuse for stopping, that one must will the mind to keep moving, pushing the pain back further and further, all the time knowing the finish line is still many hours away. Just as he draws on my physical freshness, I draw on his courage, his determination to blot out all unseen monsters trying to keep him from reaching the finish line before the clock strikes 24 hours.

Somehow David manages to come in at 23 hours and 32 minutes to earn the Silver Belt Buckle, one of the most coveted prizes in ultrarunning, awarded to those fortunate few who are able to dispatch the course in under 24 hours. Being his pacer, and seeing his eyes light up at the sight of that buckle, makes me more than determined that I must attempt this race at least once. I don't know at this time whether or not I can earn my buckle, let alone even finish the race, but I vow in my mind that I will train as I have never trained before to give it my best shot.

CHAPTER 5
FRIENDS AND SPEED AT LAST CHANCE
(43.3 MILES)

He, who, from zone to zone,
Guides through the boundless sky thy certain flight,
In the long way that I must trace alone,
Will lead my steps aright.
(William Cullen Bryant)

I leave Robinson Flat at last somewhat refreshed and begin walking up a short but gradually inclined road. Deep shadows splash across the brown, uneven dirt as the mid-morning summer sun pushes reluctantly from behind the clouds and jabs its bright, warming rays into the tall, green evergreen trees that dominate the surroundings. I quickly shove down a few bites of food and attempt to get my legs back underneath me by walking rapidly. As the road begins to level off I push my legs into an unsteady trot. Another runner about 20 yards ahead of me begins doing the same slow jog.

I know that from here to Last Chance, about 14 miles, is all either on level ground and downhill except for one, two mile section. On this forgiving portion of the course I can make up some time before encountering the giant climb out of Deadwood Canyon to Devil's Thumb, the first of three very steep canyon climbs that come in succession.

The road begins to sheer off down Cavanaugh Ridge and gets very precipitous in places. I encounter potholes everywhere on the stony, dirt pathway, and rocks are scattered randomly like an artist who has knocked over his containers of paint. There just is no pattern to the maze. I realize it is treacherous, but I run lightly and quickly, trying to make up time. I brake carefully and shift down at dangerous spots and shift into a higher gear when safety allows me to do so. My legs feel almost feathery; the normal, intense downhill pain in the quads is absent. I zip briskly by a couple of other runners and continue on my way, quickly leaving them far behind. Across a road I stride briskly and plunge down the trail on the other side. I feel strong enough to speed up even faster, but the roughness of the trail won't allow me. Safety comes first and safety means slowing down below my comfort zone. I am probably conserving extra energy by doing so.

I skid and brake to check my speed as the steepness continues. The thigh pain slowly creeps back in, and I again talk to myself out loud, warning myself to slow down and stay under control, that this is not the time to try something foolish. At the same time I can't judge how fast I am progressing, I do know that I am gaining some time on the 24 hour deadline at this point in the race. I also now run completely by myself, with no other runners in sight either in front or back of me.

The trail becomes even steeper now, and below me I hear voices as I near Deep Canyon I, an aid station set up on a wide, well kept gravel and dirt road. I half hop and half run down the embankment, skidding to check my momentum, and step out gingerly on to the road. The station is small but I refill my bottles and grab a handful of assorted food items, munching as I stand there. I have been running alone before I arrive at this station. Suddenly several runners are standing next to me getting refreshments and talking to each other with animation. Where do they all come from all of a sudden? I can't tell whether I have caught up with them or whether they have caught me while I'm stopped. Several of them take off down the road toward the next canyon with hardly a stop at all. I know I shouldn't linger here except for a few seconds.

I embark on a two mile, gradually downhill, beautifully groomed road with virtually no footing problems. My legs feel fresh from trotting downhill more slowly than I had wanted to on the last section of the trail. I begin running at an even, steady pace, but my legs say go on, pick it up. I increase my tempo slowly; I'm now beginning to fly, probably the fastest I've run all day. I'm really making time now and I feel strong, somewhat like racing during the middle of a fast marathon. I pass several runners quickly. Breathing deeply and easily, I lengthen my stride and roll on downward, relaxed and confident, around corners, cutting them tight to the inside.

Deeper and deeper into the canyon I plunge, the road curving s-like into the gulch. I approach the bottom where it starts a gradual uphill climb. Off to my left is a little stream cascading over the rocks and pooling out before entering a culvert, then racing across the dark bumpy metal to fall

The trail can become rocky in places.

out on the other side, continuing its magical journey down the mountainside. I suddenly realize that I am building up heat from the now cloudless sky with the sun bouncing its rays directly off the small stones and dirt on the road. No trees protect me on the wide road, although giant firs and pines flank the bank. The glaring heat reflects back directly into my face; sweat drips down my forehead. I brake to a sudden halt, jump quickly down by the pool, dip my scarf and hat into the cool water and throw them back on.

The sudden coolness of the water tingles my body, as water drips all over my shirt and shorts. All is still quiet on the road; no other runners appear around the corner. The only sounds are my quiet breathing and the light rushing music of the crystal clear water sliding over the slick rocks in the pool. I jump back up on the road taking another look back, still seeing no one, and slowly resume my speed down to the bottom of the hill. Sometimes when no one else is present, I feel like I'm not in any kind of race at all, only out for a solitary workout.

Just before I start uphill, the road levels off and I saunter to a jog; gravity slows me down with its pull, and I must crank up my muscles again to push myself onward. On the other side of a small bridge is an automobile with several people sitting in lawn chairs and talking: spectators or someone's crew. It is enjoyable to see someone, and I quietly acknowledge their words of encouragement.

The road begins back up the hill, with the Deep Canyon II checkpoint a couple of miles ahead. I creep back to a quick, recovery walk, but gradually and methodically other runners are gaining on and passing me, some walking faster than I am, and, yes, some even running. The red-haired woman passes me again at a fast shuffle. I must have passed her on the downhill but don't remember doing so. Finally I figure that I can outpace some of these people and break into a slow jog up the slope.

Running is not uncomfortable and the wide, dirt and pebble surface is forgiving. I jog for a few minutes until my legs begin to slightly labor rather than run without exerted effort. I again walk for a few minutes, moving with rapid, medium long strides. I return back to running again, and the run-walk sequences advance me steadily to the aid station. Groups of friendly people appear along the road, with the aid station just ahead.

Deep Canyon II, or Dusty Corners, is a relatively obscure checkpoint but one containing very enthusiastic personnel and spectators. People call me out by my hometown, and all the comments are loud and encouraging in nature. The positive feedback pumps extra adrenaline through my system, and I surge perceptively faster onward.

This station performs a couple of deeds that are different from all the other stations so far. By this time midday has arrived and the heat is building up, the wind dying down, and the sun penetrating more intensely. The temperature, however, is not as bad as it could be by now. A light, gentle breeze is still present to keep the heat from driving too deeply into my body and perhaps leaving me faint. I've trained many hours in the heat, and the warm air doesn't seem too bad. However, I'm not one to take chances with the elements, so I take advantage of their two special services.

The first one offered is a hose down. I step on a platform built like a shower stall. One person wraps a plastic cover tightly around my shoes to keep them from getting wet; how thoughtful. Another, using a nozzle on the end of a hose, sprays a fine mist from my head all the way down my body. The cold water cools my warm skin quickly and dramatically, abating my hot, sticky, body temperature. The sudden, cold shower prickles my skin and momentarily takes my breath away.

The second special help is ice put inside my cap. I wear a white biking cap, and there is not much room between my cap and the top of my head, but somehow someone jams a handful of small, chunky pieces of ice into my cap and carefully places the cap on my head, assuring me that it should last for at least a mile or so.

I grab my full bottles and stuff some crackers into my mouth, try to thank these wonderful people with my mouth full, and take off jogging down the road, my stomach slightly sloshing with fluids. For the initial time in my life the top of my head feels frozen. I've touched ice many times before, but this ice appears extra cold, like chips from a blue, arctic iceberg that has floated its way on to the trail. Ice water gradually begins to drip down the sides of my head and face, bestowing chilling relief. I touch the top of my cap and feel a giant, tingling lump. The cap bulges with the ice, and any pressure downward by my hand actually induces a small pain on the top of my head.

I'm back on the road now leading a few, gentle miles down to Last Chance, the next major medical checkpoint. I begin generously drinking water every few minutes to make sure my weight is all right at the weigh-in. With each step water sloshes inside my stomach, bouncing off my insides like waves crashing rhythmically off a sea wall. The road is comfortable, rolling and downhill, with a few minor trouble spots for footing, but generally very forgiving. I'm not sure how long it should take to get to Last Chance, but I appear to be making excellent time, striding out to the edge of pushing it hard, but backing off slightly. As I catch up and run for a moment with a fellow competitor before passing him, I tell him how great the ice feels. This type of use for ice is news to him; he apparently wasn't asked if he wanted some. Then I notice he isn't wearing a cap.

Unexpectedly I find myself running in pace with another competitor who has caught up with me. Our strides seem similar, so we run together for awhile. I introduce myself, and he tells me he is from Texas and has completed the race a couple of times under 24 hours. He says he is on his fastest early pace ever, primarily due to the cool weather. When I tell him

I'm not able to eat every much because I don't feel hungry, he discloses to me not to worry about it because food is difficult to digest during the heat of the day anyway. He indicates I should only worry about getting enough to drink. Then we stop talking and run together to Last Chance quietly together, our strides rhythmically in tune to each other, crunching and scraping gently over the dirt and rocky terrain.

I reflect back and am amazed how easy it is to make friends out here on the trail. Whether in a race or on training runs, these ultra events cement new kinds of friends, those who share in the common, hidden knowledge of the ultrarunner. These friendships made on the run are of a rare nature, often made by accident when two of us happen to run in the same place at the same time on the roads or trails. I meet and make numerous friends during the several organized training runs held on the Western States Trail, along the trails of several 50 mile races I run in preparation for the Western States, and during the race itself.

Racing friends aren't like normal friends, whom we stay close to throughout our lives and can count on to help us on an everyday basis. Racing friends are not the types of people I may continue to see or correspond with outside of racing because we live so far apart, and after the race is completed, we all go back to our normal separate lives, severed often by the great distances between our hometowns. We may encounter each other months from now at another race, but we'll always remember one another for our unique, individual thoughts, attitudes and racing abilities.

Yet out on the trail when I am running with one of my new friends, we feel free to share all our innermost thoughts and dreams, fears and problems. Perhaps we don't feel intimidated by each other because we know that afterwards we may be separated by long periods of time. Also, we are together on the course sharing the majesty of the race itself, an intimate knowledge that the competitors understand between each other through only a silent signal of comradeship. We compete but we are like brothers and sisters, and our feelings are shared like siblings. Some strong emotional therapy is often consummated on the trails.

We may also share each other's energy to keep us moving through the physical and emotional difficulties of the long, sometimes desperate hours on the course. Occupied time goes by faster, and runners' energies really do pull on our trail partners like magnets. I don't ever remember competing with anyone along the Western States Trail. If one of us feels like moving ahead or dropping back, a mute signal articulates the intention for the moment, and we separate from each other. Each of us has a long journey ahead, and we must take these journeys in our own rhythms.

On a training run, one new friend is a lawyer and talks about how frustrating his job is sometimes, that frequently he wishes he could chuck it all. Another friend is a fellow teacher who is looking for a new job. He relates to me where he would like to locate and all the interviews he must undergo. Another discusses the many hours he must spend training and how it is creating conflicts with what the rest of his family wants to do. These are people I didn't know existed a few hours ago; I suddenly meet them while clambering over a rugged, stone-littered trail, and now they comfortably talk about very personal problems and events in their lives.

The favorite topic, of course, is running, because this bond links all of us as true brothers and sisters, and is an affair of the body and soul we can all understand. It is comforting to be with someone to whom I don't have to explain why I am doing this race. I don't need to explain to these comrades in arms and spirit, because they understand, for they have the same reasons. Sometimes we talk animately about our dreams in this race and also about our fears, especially about our fears of failing because of something unlucky happening to us. Other times we don't need to talk at all, because our thoughts cross to each other through a kind of electricity from our movements, our breathing, our inner telepathy.

One runner wants only to finish in under 30 hours, because he feels he simply doesn't have the ability or speed to finish under 24 hours. His primary goal is to just keep moving to the finish. He knows he will complete the course if he is conservative and keeps a slow, steady pace. He fears that he really hasn't trained adequately for the race, a fear most runners share. Nearly all of us never feel adequately trained for this event. My friend never really talks about the act of failing itself; it is almost too painful to bring up as a topic. Yet we both know many of us in the physical presence of each other on the trail will fail to finish the race.

Another friend knows he has the ability to make it under 24 hours but is afraid that he will go out too hard. He has previously often lacked the patience, he says, and this event is his first 100 miler. From his marathon and 50 mile times, he is a definite candidate for breaking 24 hours, but he is afraid he won't hold together over the long distance. We talk about the virtues of patience, but we both know that only he can apply the concentration needed to put it together properly on race day. I often am in awe when looking at this runner because I wish I possessed his ability in my body, but I also realize that I have certain, hardy mental attributes that may get me through the race while he becomes a casualty on the battle front.

There is my friend who can and does have the ability to make it under 24 hours, but he has a miserable day as everything possibly goes wrong. His outlook is acceptance for the moment, but his confidence and determination have really grown; he has experienced the course, and he knows he will be back to win the buckle another time because he has the ability to do so. Nothing will waylay this friend who now knows he can do it if no one thing fails him because his failure tells him it is possible. His dream is not desperate at all; he knows it can be attained.

My most poignant friend has a desperate dream of finishing the race in a blaze of glory under 24 hours and becoming a hero in his own eyes and in the eyes of his family and friends. I see the theme in my friend's eyes and hear it in his voice. He truly believes he can win the belt buckle, but brutal, stark reality is staring at him with unending hostility in its wake. This blatant actuality says that there is no way that he will finish before 5 a.m. the next morning; all the training he can cram into his hours and days won't help him at this point.

My friend is desperate for the buckle and has trained months for it, knowing in his own mind he can accomplish the immense deed. For whatever reason, nature says to this person's body that it is not physically possible because the ability is not present and never will be. The mind is willing to get the buckle, but the body just does not have the capacity to make it in time.

Maybe this is the friend that race is really all about. He will fail to finish or will finish under 30 hours, satisfied for the moment with the plaque. When the furor of the attempt is over, his optimism will soon return, and he will tell me and others that he will be back again and accomplish the goal then. His dream never leaves him; without it his life has less meaning. Often he will try numerous times and continue to fail, but his optimism remains; all he needs is better training and more determination. But maybe just once, on that perfect day with his body in perfect shape, with no physical problems detaining him anywhere during the race, with grit and determination, he will realize his dream. This ending to my friend's story has happened in victory more than once. My friend's human spirit may take him beyond mere mortals, and he will reach the pedestal of his nirvana.

I wish that all of my new friends are successful. Unfortunately all but a couple of them fail to finish the race because the demons lying in wait for them jump up and knock them off their quests. The next day at the awards ceremony I see two of them who tell me what happened to them, and they indicate they will be back for another attempt. They presently seem quietly resigned to their failures. The others I don't see again after the race and have no idea what happened to them. I do know that I inevitably will see them lined up again sometime in a future race ready for a new challenge, the spirit of determination etched once more on their faces.

One of my new running friends does make it under 24 hours. Urgently charging the last remaining hills and constantly glancing at his watch, he tells me made it to the finish line in 23 hours and 55 minutes. I see tired, courageous happiness etched in his face. His friends are joyous for him, but only the two of us can quietly and intimately share the agonies and mental anguishes he has just gone through. All I can tell him is that it is a gutsy performance; we both know exactly what I mean. How can you measure the heart in a person?

I have run for several steady miles now with my friend from Texas. Since he is a veteran of the Western States, I try to discuss strategy with him on how he is able to get under 24 hours. Even with all the brain picking I've done before the race, and all the planning I've done, I learn a couple of valuable lessons from my new running partner. It doesn't bother him to share the reasons for his success in past races, because I'm sure he would genuinely like to see me succeed, even though he hasn't met me until now. I listen to him and watch his stride, how he handles the uphills and downhills. A couple of minor points he makes definitely make sense to me, and I store them in the back of my mind for later use in the race.

With my mind relaxed and wandering a bit, I now think only of each step and really nothing else. I consciously reflect to myself that I am surprised that I feel so well at this point. Suddenly I am aware that we are approaching the Last Chance aid station, so much sooner than I remembered it in my practice run. I am either running much faster than I think I am, but more likely I overestimated the actual distance from the last aid station. This progress is very encouraging, but I remember to gulp down most of my water and pour the remainder on my head and shoulders before reaching the scale.

I hop on the scale with what feels to be about a pound of ice still under my cap, with the top of the head still feeling like a popsicle. My weight checks out two pounds over my beginning weight; it is no wonder with all that extra ice figured in. Someone asks me how I feel, and I respond with a positive, solitary phrase. I step down from the scale and grab a couple of saltines, munching on one, and putting one in my pack for later use. I gulp down some coke and make sure my bottles are full to the top. I now continue onward alone, my friend having gone on ahead down a gentle road toward the first of the three successive deep canyons. At the bottom I will encounter a couple of miles of switchbacks up the other side, a period of walking and recovery of all the muscles used during the downhill section.

This is my first really tough test since Duncan Canyon. Physically I am ready to blast down the tight, steep switchbacks to the bottom, and mentally I feel ready to take on the brutal uphill portion on the other side. Running momentarily down the road before the trail drops off into the canyon, I pick up with my running friend again. I feel thankful that I have come this far without any major problems, still on an easy sub-24 hour pace and feeling great. I know the race is getting ready to start in earnest.

I know that I am a marginal candidate for the buckle, but I also perceive that on race day I will be at my ultimate peak, with miles and miles of rigorous training behind me, both physically and mentally toughened for whatever lies ahead. This will be no cheap attempt, and I will have really dedicated myself for my mission. I'm not going to seek the buckle; I'm going to attempt to do the best job I can possibly manage.

My main goal in the race is not to win the buckle; my primary goal is to give the best performance I can for 100 miles. If finishing or the buckle is not the outcome of my best performance, I will have no excuses. I resolve that when my race is concluded, no matter what the ending, I can acknowledge that I have done my very best and will be fulfilled.

I send in my application again and begin training the first week in December, even though I haven't been accepted yet. If I don't attain entry, I will use my training for other ultra races. But I have a gut feeling that this is my year. Late in December I receive a letter in the mail from the

Western States committee. As I read the fateful words of acceptance, a warm comfortable sensation fills my body. From now to race day, I will turn into a different runner. The race is over six months away, but my race begins that day in December.

The letter is in my hands. It is too late to turn back now; my date with destiny is set - June 28, 1986. I presently acknowledge that I must face it head on. I accept that fact, and I know I will be ready on race day. I will be 43 years old when the gun goes off on that early Saturday morning.

CHAPTER 6
BRUTAL CANYON TO DEVIL'S THUMB
(47.8 MILES)

Pain has an element of blank;
It cannot recollect
When it begun, or if there were
A day when it was not.

It has no future but itself,
Its infinite contain
Its past, enlightened to perceive
New periods of pain.
(Emily Dickinson)

I feel at the pinnacle of my racing form as I depart Last Chance with my new running friend and glide down the road to my rendezvous with the first of the killer canyons, the North Fork of the Middle Fork of the American River. I will then advance back up to that most evil sounding landmark, Devil's Thumb. We run swiftly along the relatively smooth, almost rock free road, when gradually the road becomes rough and eventually shifts to a trail; the sudden drop begins.

The trail is mildly smooth with only a few obstacles of small stones and roots embedded into the packed dirt. Many trees angle high above our heads on the flank of the precipitous canyon wall. The limbs provide a portion of the trail with welcome shade. The tops of tall trees growing lower on the slope sway at eye level as we run. The weather is still quite cool and clear, as a gentle but refreshing breeze continues to rustle through the branches and needles of the trees and across the trail singing its gentle, rhythmic, ancient melody. The cooling effect of the smooth, steady zephyrs gently tingles and relieves the hot stickiness and comfortable, rancid smell of the sweat forming on my body. Leaves and scattered debris of broken limbs and loose rocks litter the trail in some places.

I plummet down the very steep incline, letting my thighs release their tension as I barrel just under control on the smooth grade. I brake slightly as I approach a rough, rocky spot, pick my way carefully over the rocks with my eyes glued to my feet, and jettison the flow just before I get to the smooth dirt on the other side. I charge in abandon once more, but suddenly look up and apply my brakes again, pumping furiously to make the steep 180 degree switchback turn. I try to stay with my friend but am slowly falling behind, but only by a few seconds each minute we run together. We zip past a couple of slowly moving fellow runners with barely a hello exchanged. I find myself chasing my running friend down the narrow ribbon of switchbacks, losing ground slowly. His energy flow is tugging me down the mountainside.

The trail descends the opposite direction, and a moment later I encounter yet another switchback, then yet another and another. They wind downward like a coiled snake ready at any moment to strike out and grab my thighs and knees. I am dropping fast and pounding hard across dirt, rocks, and old leaves, my gut feeling rising in my throat like a sinking elevator. My quads now ache piercingly with each jarring foot strike, but I know if I can get to the bottom I will find relief on the level and uphill. I can hear the water rush of fast snow-melt below me as I drop deeper and deeper into the chasm. Perhaps it is the cousin of the trail water I crossed earlier in the day, seeking out its relative in an eventual meeting at the wide river deep in the earth canyon.

I wonder if I'll be able to get out of this pit. All this downhill means an abundance of very steep uphill, struggling to reach back to the sky again. I clamber over an old slide area, the hillside opening up, trees blown away from some winter avalanche, powerless to resist, as I am powerless to stop my rapid descent. A new trail has been carved through the mass of tangled, giant boulders and hillside debris, the path staggering across the clearing. I quickly but gingerly negotiate the sun-baked, uneven, hot trail surface. Straight down below me to the left several hundred feet is a smooth, sparkling stream, giving off its hues of greens and blues, with the sun reflecting white off its rushing rapids. I descend on deeper into the waiting arms of the canyon depths.

I have practiced countless hours at my downhill running in preparation for this moment. I know fast downhill running is a technique essential to finishing the Western States, as during the course of the event I go down slopes which added together produce a loss of over 22,000 feet of elevation. I imagine starting at the top of some snow capped Himalayan peak and running down like a madman all the way to sea level, and the enormity of the descent begins to sink in. Somehow I must negotiate all of this, and the terrain ranges from gentle to very steep, from smooth dirt to the roughest, rocky surface imaginable with loose, trail rubble sliding down the mountain along with my skidding legs.

Normal running articles advise the reader that hill training is an important element in a runner's development, but the emphasis is usually on the techniques of running the uphill portion. The runner is told to run hard up the hills to gain maximum benefit but to take it easy on the downhills because hard downhill running is damaging on the legs.

For the ultrarunner the emphasis is on running the downhills hard because this is the one segment of trail racing where the runner can make up time. The race course dictates such running and those who face blown thighs and knees will forever fail to reach the finish line. I practice running downhills diligently and hard, gradually building up to where my legs and knees can handle these sections with comfortable ease. I know I must have my downhill muscles trained to run all the 22,000 feet and survive them with a minimum of pain. I practice power walking on the steep uphills for this is what I must do on the uphills most of the time during the actual race.

I use different downhill techniques depending on the steepness of the trail, the condition of the surface, and how well I am enduring at that particular moment. I burn up the time on the gradual downhills over smooth, dirt trails. I let my legs stretch out, grabbing for a relaxed but quick shuffling stride, barely letting my shoes clear the ground. I move for a steady tempo, one that won't tire me out quickly. I instinctively adjust this tempo slightly when the pitch of the trail makes a minor change. This moment of running is my strong point, and with many hours of practice time behind me before the race, I know I won't burn myself out because my hill muscles are equipped for the event. Relief is usually close by anyway because at the bottom of a hill, I usually start uphill again, and I then use my quick, steady walking to recover.

The trail now gets a little rocky, but remains a steady drop. I slow myself down ever so slightly to avoid falling over the myriad of stones that clutter the pathway. I shorten my stride, exaggerate lifting my knees higher than usual like I'm running on eggs, and then concentrate on putting down each foot plant like I'm stepping on a freshly waxed floor. A sudden smooth spot of a few yards lets me speed up the tempo for several precious seconds. I talk out loud to myself, telling me not to do anything foolish, not to be in a hurry and rage out of control. One negligent misstep and I may find myself suddenly sprawled out on the trail, cut up with a painful and potential race-fatal sprain or muscle pull. I stir reluctant caution with abandoned caution; the notes of my tune must be blended together in harmony. I have practiced this type of running many times, so I know how to push it to the brink of disaster without falling off the edge. If I take a side in my abandon it is on the side of safety. I still have miles to go before I reach the finish, and I want to reach it intact.

The trail diverts to only dirt now and is generally smooth, but it suddenly drops down steeper into a canyon. I slam on the brakes to help control my speed so I don't barrel down completely out of control. My quads and knees fight the pressure of gravity, anchoring my body against free fall. Out of control means danger, but this is when my lower extremities begin to hurt. I know that when I reach an uphill portion of the trail, I will have to walk to recover because I have done this many times before. I spread my legs a little wider for balance and try to let them roll as much as I can. The legs keep yelling back at me to stop or let them release the pressure and allow my body to go completely in an abandoned coast. My mind says not to, so I continue to take choppy steps with a wide base.

I barely pick up my feet, just enough to clear the obstacles. My legs are almost straight, my knees bent just slightly enough to lift my legs. I do a trail shuffle, a sort of mystic dance, conserving energy but putting myself right on the brink of being upended by a rock or a root. Again my eyes are riveted to the trail, darting wildly and intensely for any rock or branch that might jump up like some alive demon of the woods and bite me with a poison that my body may not be able to reject.

The trail is a series of steep switchbacks, descending like a wild unending Z down deeper and deeper into the seemingly bottomless pit. I blast it hard to the next corner. A few feet from the corner I begin my braking until I almost stop, dust spewing in little swirls around my naked legs, now baked brown by the sun and soil. I carefully negotiate around the corner, taking little baby steps; a quick turn could propel me off the bank. I round the bend and turn on the afterburners along the next open stretch. I repeat the procedure over and over as I propel myself down the side of the mountain trying to beat some invisible opponent to the wedge of the terrain at the bottom. I am under control; even though my thighs hurt slightly I know relief is just ahead when I reach the lowest point and switch muscles to start my walk up the other side. I converse with myself quietly out loud to keep me concentrating on every step, all the way to the bottom of the canyon, not letting up for even one split second moment.

I reach the crest of a steep hill, and it is now time to go back down. The trail suddenly drops off in a steep, uncompromising angle that I should never walk, let alone run. Twigs, rocks of all sizes and angles, and humps of dirt litter the trail like a painter who has just dropped and spilled his entire box of paints and brushes. The dirt is almost ankle deep as I start down; my legs can absolutely not take it running. I brake harder and shift into a compound low gear, leaning back at an awkward angle, causing even more pain to my thighs and knees. I skid down the hill, holding on to the brink of disaster even more closely than ever. I talk to myself again, this time a little louder with words that even I don't hear or understand. I can't go out of control; it could mean an ankle or a knee, or a trip and stumble and a head first dive down the hill and the end of my race. I even turn my body and shuffle sideways down the bank.

I run down the hills. But one hill isn't like any other hill. I know this when I train, and I know it on the race trail. I cope with it the best I can, use speed when I must, employ caution when it is needed. The most discouraging kind of hill is the downhill that I reach after an uphill walk that is so steep that I have to walk down it. Where is justice ever served? It is supposed to be time to gain time, not to lose more of it.

I am a downhill runner, and I enjoy it whenever I can. Gravity is my friend; speed is my ally. I bask in my friendship with the downhill, and I use it to finish my long race. I may cry at times during a descent, a cry of pain and frustration. However, I truly know that this ally of mine, although it may be tough on me, is really the reason for my success. I work with it, not against it. I haven't pampered my friend in practice, and now in the race itself, I can use it to full advantage. I make it a crucial part of my racing success.

I finally slide down the last steep portion of the trail and see the bridge ahead and directly below me through the thick evergreens, a solidly built foot structure high above the water, a link that spans the width of the beautifully flowing river. The water below flows quickly and symphonically in a never ending rush to its own finishing line in the canyon bottom. What a great view, but I haven't got time to really stop and look.

I have a long journey up the other side. Before the climb arrives I jog gently and slowly along a short portion of level trail flanked by deep, lush vegetation and overhanging ferns. A small, cool stream spills down a man-high dirt bank singing its hushed, endless one note song as it emerges from the lush vegetation. The water sloshes across the trail, leaving a smooth, pastoral pool at the base of the bank. My running friend has already wet down all his clothing and while sitting down, leans back into the pool, submerging his entire upper body into the chilly water. He jerks back up, letting out a rush of air, cool fluid glistening on his skin and shirt, his hair wildly unkempt with dripping water.

I dip my cap and bandanna into the water, lift them out and replace them. The sudden cold instantaneously shoots a spine tinging shock through my head and shoulders, spreading downward inside my legs. I dip my cupped hands into the water and pour the cold, clear liquid over the top of my head and on to my chest until my upper body is soaked and my sweat smell is concealed. The whole process temporarily takes my breath away, but I know this will be the last such pleasure I will experience until I reach the top of Devil's Thumb, about a 45 minute walk up the steep mountainside.

Another runner hurriedly throws a handful of water on his face in passing and glances at us with a strange look. What's his hurry, I wonder? I realize I must soon depart from this paradise, so I straighten up my body, adjust my waist pack, and begin walking slowly up the hill. I strangely encounter a little trouble gathering my breath as I push upward, and my legs are a little heavy, but they soon loosen up with repetitive walking strides. I am slow and methodical in my steps. I pick up one leg and firmly plant my foot on a secure spot in the path, transfer my weight to that lead foot, pushing downward, straightening my leg using the power of my thighs for the next step. The straight leg powers me up one more short gain toward the pinnacle of the mountain. I repeat the act slowly and consistently, hundreds of times in rhythm with the changing steepness of the thin ribbon of the trail and its switchbacks winding among the stately, majestic pine and fir trees lining the side of the trail.

Soon my friend catches up to me by using a quicker walking stride and passes me. As I stroll up the mountainside, he gradually lengthens his lead, and soon, after many miles of being together, he just seems to disappear into the shadowy woods, and I never see him again. Much later after the finish of the race, I look for his name and discover he finished in 23 hours and 24 minutes. Thanks for your help, Luke Barber.

Somewhere near the middle of the race.

These shadows make the walk cooler and easier than walking in the open, sunny glare. I can actually hear the birds chirping in the cave-like lush, dark green vegetation, and I hear an occasional voice reverberate something unintelligible below me on the side of the mountain, an echo from another runner several switchbacks below me. I look below my feet and see another walker two switchbacks below me. He can't see me from his perspective, and I feel power over him from my misinterpretation of the distance between us. The trail is several feet wide and actually very smooth, an old trail worn down from many years and many feet gently crossing its surface. By overall standards, the trail is a freeway, occasionally marred by a rough spot of rocky surface.

I am now aware vaguely of only one item, my watch, for I don't want to look up to see how much more distance I have to cover. All I know is that in about 45 minutes I'll be there. The legs don't seem to like this 45 minute idea and start begging to slow down, but I keep pumping my arms to add power to my faltering strides.

At the end of a straight section beginning a switchback, I encounter another runner struggling up the trail, his leg in obvious pain, another smaller runner helping him. I recognize the injured runner as Baz Hawley, a well known ultra race director and runner, and he says his Achilles tendon is injured. The other runner then turns around, and I recognize him as Steve Warshawer, one the country's supreme ultrarunners, who is obviously having an awful day as he finished third in the race the year previous. I stare at both of them for a moment before asking if I can do anything to help. They tell me there is nothing I can do so I continue trudging onward, energized by knowing that even the best can falter. It can happen to anyone at any time.

I do slow down occasionally and even stop twice for about ten seconds to catch my breath, which seems to be troubled by the over abundance of liquid in my stomach. I can even hear the fluid sloshing around inside like someone jiggling a half full thermos. I keep sipping on a plastic bottle full of water, aware that another weigh station is at the top of the canyon. Finally, as I range higher and higher, I see sky above me, and I look up to see the dreaded but welcome landmark off to my left that tells me I'm near the top, a rock outcropping that looks like a huge thumb, which was given the appropriate name of Devil's Thumb. Is this steep trail thumbing its nose at me, or is it trying to give me the thumbs up because I'm near the top? Maybe it is a false thumbs up, since it belongs to the devil. Perhaps it isn't a thumb at all but an index finger.

I reach the top, stumbling and jogging my way over to the aid station. In a timeless rerun of other stops many people are there to greet me, but the crews are further on down a mile or so. An official takes my belt and leads me to the scale. I step on it and see that my weight is exactly the same as my starting weight again; it should be with all the water I'm pouring into my seemingly bottomless pit. Things are still going well in that category.

I continue down the trail another mile with people lined up everywhere on both sides waiting for their runners and cheering on anyone else they see. Finally I observe one of my crew ahead in our club's familiar green

T-shirt, and he comes out to lead me to where my crew has set up my chair. It is 19 miles since I last saw them and their familiar smiling faces look fabulous to me; also they tell me all at once that I look great even though I know I must look like hell by now. I have finally arrived at the Deadwood aid station.

I go through the procedures now familiar of changing socks and eating and drinking. Food begins to taste more and more like dry paste; I take a couple of swigs of my fruit-blended mix and stuff some salty chips into my mouth and munch furiously. I don't really know why I brought so much extra food; I surely won't be able to eat it all. My crew busily tries to get me ready in five minutes to put me back on the trail again. I tell them to fill one bottle with Max and the other with water. The Max drink is helping, I think, but it is beginning to have a bland, sickening taste like everything else I consume.

There are crews everywhere along the road with runners coming in and leaving and an abundance of loud talking and some shouting. The setting in the woods is almost pastoral, and the sounds of humanity echo through the tall trees. I really do feel fairly stable at this stage, almost half way into the race. Except for the problem with getting my breath coming up the hill, I feel strong, especially in the legs. The quads are a little stiff, but no more than would be expected at this juncture in the race. In addition, I have finished the first of three tough successive canyons.

Someone on my crew informs me that it is time to get up and leave. I rise, put on my waist belt, making sure my bottles are secure, check for any last minute items I may need, thank my crew, and prepare to leave. I tell them I'll be looking forward to seeing them at Michigan Bluff after another six miles, and then I take off in a slow, stiff jog, turning around to wave goodbye.

As I head on down the road, I realize that I am about to embark on the deepest and perhaps toughest section of the course, according to many, the deep El Dorado Canyon, during the middle and the hottest part of the afternoon. I mentally steel myself as I jog down the road toward the drop off. I won't look at the depth of the canyon itself. I have two goals, first to run as fast as I can to the bottom along the long, descending trail, and, second, to walk the long trip back up the other side without trying to hurry. It is a repeat of the last canyon, only not with quite the same flavor and texture. With another deep breath, I begin my charge down the side of the canyon.

Life is full of ironies. Growing up in a small community in the mountains I was interested in all the different sports that were available to me, all except one. That one was running. I never did enjoy running for the joy of the sport itself. I enjoyed sports like baseball, football, tennis, skiing, and even the woodman's sports of fishing and hunting. But running track was out of the question, and apparently long distance running hadn't been invented yet, at least not in my environment.

With all the athletic adventures I tried and enjoyed over the years, it wasn't until I was 37 years old that I discovered a calling that had been waiting for me all these years. Long distance running became a special joy, something where I could get away from the rest of world and kick back and become my own hero. I enjoyed running with others who enjoyed the sport, but what I really looked forward to was the solitary run away from everyone and everything.

As a child I did enjoy getting out into the woods and playing games, of exploring trails and places where there were no trails. Vivid in my mind is the time my friends and I were flying kites and I had my kite extended far over the canyon behind my house. The string broke and the kite disappeared on the opposite canyon wall. My friends and I then spent the rest of the day in an adventure of finding that kite in a place we probably shouldn't have ventured.

I remember the times the family went deer hunting in some remote part of the state. We would take off before dark on a freezing November morning and start our hikes across the wooded terrain looking for our prey. It wasn't killing the buck that I remember so vividly. What still stands out is the walk itself, the quiet and the peace of the woods. I vividly recall being lost for a couple of hours and the complete isolation and loneliness that I felt at the time. Yet I felt a calming peace of being alone with nature, with no contact to the outside world.

I now understand that long distance running, and especially running on the trails, had been just waiting all these years for me to find it. In a logical extension of my early years ultrarunning became the perfect sport for me and what I was meant to do for as long I could do it.

CHAPTER 7
CRITICAL MOMENT AT MICHIGAN BLUFF
(55.7 MILES)

Life isn't equal. Living with humiliation is
part of not being equal to everyone. In few fields
of struggle are the standards of excellence so clearly
worked out for our humiliation. Being humbled
is the name of - some game or other.

(Michael Novak)

El Dorado Canyon: the words strike fear into the hearts of all of us. From Devil's Thumb/Deadwood I take off for the deepest canyon on the course, knowing that I must do it comfortably and make it in one piece into Michigan Bluff, a long, difficult six miles away.

I run easily but quickly on the nice, gently flowing, dirt road down the ridge. The jog is an easy warmup before the canyon descent. The terrain is relatively flat and the trail gentle and forgiving. It gives me a perfect tuneup for the challenge ahead. The road bends sharply to the right; the trail drops off abruptly to the left, a sign warning of a hazardous trail section ahead, and I begin the venture downward into the canyon. The trail here is a series of switchbacks just like the last canyon, except they are not so steep here and much longer. The trail is packed dirt smooth, the weather is still cool, and the trees give some welcome shade. I stretch out my stride and my pace quickens; I begin gaining ground at a highly increased tempo, the warm, early afternoon air sifting quickly across my sweat-stained skin.

Each section before the next switchback seems to go on forever. But these sections are gentle and downhill, and it is time to go rapidly, to pound it out a little, letting the brakes loose to coast to the brink of losing control. Some parts never seem to end, and I feel like I'm making no progress down the hillside. All the distance I gain is around the side of the hill. Finally the trail reverses direction 180 degrees, and I begin the run back to the other side of the hill, a little lower than when I started the last straight section.

I advance deeper and deeper into the canyon back and forth along the hillside until my thighs begin to ache a deep burn, but I must not stop or slow down yet. One stretch with the canyon wall to my right goes on for a time that seems like eternity. First I encounter dry trail vegetation, small brown leaves and twigs littering the trail. The grasses and plants are a combination of dead tan mixed with the weak green of struggling life. The soil is bone dry. I need to make up as much time as possible here before I get to the bottom because I know I must walk up the other side. I keep pouring in the liquid to keep hydrated, and my stomach and chest seem bloated from all the fluids sloshing around inside of me. An uncomfortable tightness grabs at me, and it affects my breathing slightly, just enough to let me know when I happen to pick up the pace too suddenly.

The grasses begin to turn deeper green now. I run across a small spring trickling out of a small pipe, pooling up, and then cascading down the mountainside, its clear, cool, virgin water first gurgling slowly and gently across the trail. I attack the water briefly with my bandana and cap, the water pouring down my head and upper body as I replace the bandana around my neck and the cap back on my head. My skin tingles with pleasure, and I breathe quickly and jerkily to get fresh, clean air into my lungs.

Down and down I tumble across the mountainside. The greenness turns back to brown as the water disappears. I almost tiptoe across the scattered, undisciplined patterns of stones and stacks of dirt that are now hurriedly packed into a semblance of a trail. I can faintly see the water far below me, so far to go, yet not so far as heights make distances seem longer than they really are. I keep my head down concentrating on my foot placement, for each step is crucial at this speed. The burning in my legs accelerates a little, but I go on without slowing down, pushing the pace a bit more; relief will be at the bottom of the canyon.

Finally after a seemingly endless, futile struggle I get near the bottom as the trail suddenly steepens for one last precipitous drop. Uneven, steep terrain greets my aching quads. Leaning backwards to break my slide, I gingerly chop my steps down the curving embankment, my eyes carefully searching ahead of each upcoming foot strike for the next solid grip. Hard, driving pain grabs my tightened thighs as they firm up to support each downhill stride. My toes jam into the fronts of my shoes as I slam on the brakes with each stride.

I glance downward and see a short, narrow bridge directly below me now to my right. I hear voices across the bridge; Mo's aid station with its rubber swimming pool of water is near, one of the smallest yet most important aid stations on the course because it comes just before the

Runners are warned of a hazardous trail section as they enter El Dorado Canyon.

longest, steepest climb during the entire race, other than the beginning. I slide down the last little hill and the people there greet me warmly and douse me with ice cold stream water. I fumble to get the bottles off my pack, and someone replenishes them with fresh liquid. I will need every drop before I get the almost three miles to the top. When I get to Michigan Bluff, I will have another weight check, one of the most crucial medical checkpoints on the entire course. I know that climbing the upcoming section is a time to conserve myself by walking, to rest my battered body, even if I lose some precious time to my 24 hour pace. I have just made up good time coming down the slope; I will make up more time later on in the race. Now is the time to store my energy for future use.

The climb begins. From my previous training run I know it will take between 45 minutes to an hour, and I'll be happy to make it to the top in one hour. I must brace myself to be conservative and not try to rush. That can be done on other parts of the course, but not on this climb. I don't ever look up to see how far I have to go, because there are too many false tops and then shattered hopes when the hill continues upward again. Lighted sky above the trail also gives false hopes as the trail continues upwards around the hill. That perceived, apparent leveling of the pathway is only a lure to make me think I have reached the crest. I consult only my clock, knowing how much time I have left before I reach the top. Timing is the best and most accurate indicator of distance at this point.

Uphill moving is an art, a technique that will mean ultimate success to the ultrarunner. Smart slow runners don't run the uphills in a 100 miles trail run; they walk. I am not too proud to walk the uphill sections. I will run the uphills during a 10K race, a half marathon, and even a marathon, but I will walk them during a 100 miler. I can run an uphill and then recover on the downhill portion in a short race. I may feel recovered in a 100 miler, but later on in the ghostly night, somewhere out of the gloomy and shadowy desperation of the dark, the piper will come out of the brush and ask my why I ran those earlier uphills, and he will jerk my aching legs out from under me.

I actually anticipate somewhat eagerly the steep uphills at times, especially after a long downhill section of accelerated running. I blast the downhills, letting gravity and my unbound energy do the easy work. I may suffer some pain doing so in the quads and the knees, but it is a gentle pain, one that subsides on the forgiving uphills. I walk and enjoy the surroundings, patient and steady, knowing time is flying and that I'm probably not moving fast enough, but also knowing I will catch up later to the overall pace of the course. It always becomes later, and I don't worry now about my lack of speed. I tromp on, gently and lightly as possible, placing one foot in front of the other, pushing off firmly but effortlessly to the next step.

I walk in somewhat of a hurry, but I am never harried; I am not a race walker. If I feel tired, I back off a little and slow down. What is the rush at this point? Those who blast by me now with their images and egos flying in the wind will die later, and I'll hand them rain checks as I go by, still moving in tempo with the terrain.

That is the key, my body handling the tempo of the terrain. The steepness dictates how quickly I move. The decision isn't mine, just as my speed isn't mine to make, but instead goes to the decision of the course. The trail and the mountains make those decisions for me. I move slowly but steadily, my breathing a little labored, but my legs feel light and stable. My breath comes back to me, but my legs will not if they are burned up. Like I do while running, I increase my walking tempo slightly, reaching the brink of pain and exhaustion, then backing into my comfort zone. I conquer the mountain but under my terms and the contract I have made with the mountain.

The hillside steepens and I shift gears, slowing down. I power step, planting my foot solidly, forcing my weight down and decisively straightening my leg. I push off upward and forward, my weight absorbed by my bones, thus giving my muscles respite. I move with a slow, choppy gracefulness, almost like someone tiptoeing away from a crime scene, my body bobbing up and down with each exaggerated step.

I lift my head and look about for a moment as I keep my walking rhythm. I am high on the canyon wall, having made tremendous progress in such a short time. Headway always seems further on a steep hill than on the flat. Distances try to deceive me; short distances seem much longer than they really are. Depth perception cons me into thinking I have gone further than I really have. Distance on a flat plane seems enormous. Looking downward or upward clarifies the exact reference points of the distance, making it seem closer than it actually is.

I conquer many hills in my running, but few conquer me because I use my best attribute to get up them, patience. I know it doesn't take brute physical strength to get up the hill; it takes patience. Without it, I blast up a hill and I convince myself I really am near the top of the hill as I see sky behind the branches of hillside trees. I am high on the slope so I believe I must be near the top. Around the next corner I am sure I will be there so I increase my tempo for one final surge. I round the corner and look up, and all I behold is more hill. I have disdained patience and made a hurried and perhaps potentially fatal guess.

By not blasting and guessing I will reach the true top in all due time. I walk firmly but concentrate only on the next step, the next rock, the next angular turn on the trail. The top does not disappear; it waits in the stillness of centuries for me at the end of my long upward journey.

I am a hero when I run, along the flats, down the gentle and steep hills. I briskly settle into my pace, striding as easily as my strength will carry me. At the checkpoints, I hasten jauntily into the crowd, looking like I'm out for a Sunday jog. The air shifts by me in gentle breezes, lifting my spirits.

Walking up the hills, I am no hero. It is not the time to be heroic. I am no hero to myself for those moments of walking. Others may see me, but they are other runners turned walkers, and they understand for they stop being heroes for a moment and are doing the same thing, the smart ones anyway. My crew can't see me now, struggling, but progressing undamaged to the top of the hill and the checkpoint, where I can resume being a hero again, again for all to see.

I can take the hills forever this way, meeting the mountain face to face, but agreeing on the guidelines that get me across the finish line. When it comes to long distances, I am a hill walker all the way to the finish line.

Back on the course I feel a strange phenomenon now while climbing this particular hill. My legs are strangely very strong and powerful; there is absolutely no pain whatsoever. I feel like I'm taking an easy stroll in the woods, but I have already done over 50 miles. At the same time, I can't progress very quickly because I am winded. I have trouble catching my breath as I stroll and pull upward along the footpath; I have to stop and pause occasionally. Several other runners walking at a faster pace pass me, but I let them go for now. The bloated feeling is affecting my breathing; my lungs feel like those of an out of shape drunkard, but my legs hardly seem attached to my body. I seem to be only observing their movement onward with a blank mind. This is recovery time, and I don't need to make up time here.

I keep going and time strangely seems to pass rapidly. I don't really ponder anything, except how pleasureful it will be to see my crew at the top. I must appear full of vitality and act cheerfully to get quickly through the medical check. I know I can do that, for I feel excellent at this point. Once in a while I do glance across the canyon to the other side, marveling in the fact that I just recently ran down that canyon wall. The fact that it seems so far away encourages me even more, when I realize that I have come so far in such a relatively short period of time.

Suddenly I reach an open area and I realize the crest is near, only a few more running steps ahead. The ending to my next quest is just moments away, the pinnacles of hours of hard physical and mental labor. There is no tree cover here, and the reflection of the sun off the brown dirt creates penetrating heat, but I know Michigan Bluff is just above me. The sweat off my head and cap has a familiar, hot musty smell. Manzanita and other brush tower over my head alongside a fairly wide, gully streaked, smooth, but dusty trail. Occasional small pines and firs stick their rods of trunks through the dominating bushes.

I see some people on the side of the trail. It begins to level off now, and for the first time in nearly an hour I begin to run on the curvy, narrow trail through the brush several hundred yards to Michigan Bluff. I gulp down all the water left in my bottles, feeling like an inflated balloon, belching as I run. I pass a runner who has just passed me by running up the last part of the hot hill. He is now walking.

Michigan Bluff: it is Robinson Flat revisited in volume and enthusiasm. The road smooths out suddenly, and I see people up ahead. I round the corner to the left to cheers and boisterous activity and raise my fist in the air in an okay sign. Once again someone grabs my pack, I step quickly on the scale, and my weight is checked. It is by miracle right on my starting weight. Invisible voices ask me how I feel, and I say I'm fine, that I feel better than expected at this point. A woman at the scale tells me enthusiastically that she will bet on me making it to the finish. I try to act better than I feel, but she sees so many runners go by and must really feel I'm in comparatively good shape. Her encouragement boosts my own confidence immensely. Maybe, I realize, she says the same thing to every runner.

The medical people leave me to my crew and the aid station personnel. I've made it in relatively good condition past the most critical checkpoint on the course and I'm jubilant. Once again my crew goes through the rituals of my pit stop. They are really excited this time on how well I appear. They tell me I'm on a great pace; they should have seen me walking for an hour. I leave my pack with them for the next six miles. I will not carry it so they can get it prepared for the night portion of the course when I arrive at Foresthill. Not wearing it will give my back and hips a needed break from the constant strain from the weight of the pack. It isn't a major difference from wearing it, but every little break is important now because it may make a difference later on when I'm really exhausted.

While resting I look up at the activity around me and notice vehicles jammed everywhere, others trying to find parking places. People are walking in every direction; a hubbub of activity reigns all about me, a sort of frantic quiet. Congestion litters the road, with crews, race officials, spectators, and of course the runners. I listen to my crew talk but don't hear much, preparing myself mentally for the next six miles, the only section of the course I have never run. At least, I will encounter an original adventure before reaching the spot where I began my pacing last year.

After five minutes of sitting, eating, drinking, and changing socks and shirt, I am ready to depart. I take two full bottles in my hands and head out to Volcano Canyon, knowing that in less than an hour and a half, I will pick up my pacer, Rob. I've been waiting for a long time to have his company, which will make the journey easier; I never think human companionship can be so important. Now it becomes the next important objective in the race.

After high school the part of my life leading up to the start of my running adventures can be divided into three parts. First is attending college and lasting through the rigors of five years to earn my teaching credential. I take on my first teaching job with enthusiasm, trying to challenge high school students who are only a few years younger than I am. However, it is in the middle of the Vietnam conflict and I get a bad draft number. As soon as the school year is over I am forced to go into the service, something that I never really wanted to do.

I enter the Army and spend two years in Alaska, far away from the battlefield. I feel fortunate to be able to hide in such a comfortable spot, but there is always that hidden fear that I will called to fields of conflict. During those two years of rigorous service in the far north, I hone my skills and my deep love for the great outdoors, and I find have an uncommon ability to endure and take on the challenges of nature, especially the winters. Learning to ski at an early age, I ski the Alaskan slopes during the winter in my spare time and go fishing several times in the summer.

However, the main thing I learn is the endurance of the mind, the mental challenge of lasting the period of time before I can return to regular life. It is almost as if time has stopped, as if the rest of the world has passed me by. Each day passes slowly, but with the passing of each day, time slowly gains ground so that eventually the final bell rings and I can return to civilian life. Later on in my long endurance runs I see the parallel of patience that I must have to complete my long runs. Just as each step and each aid station puts me closer to the finish, so did each week and month propel me closer to end of my service time. It is this patience that becomes a strong part of my psyche. Nothing worthwhile, I learn, can happen quickly.

The third part of my life is getting a teaching job after I leave the service, one which begins a long run that totally engulfs my life in everything I do. The career continues during my running and lasts until just a few years ago. Once again my patience is tested and I learn to overcome the difficulties and frustrations of trying to do the best job I can.

During that period of time I discover the pleasures of long distance running and my life takes a complete turn. I now learn many new life lessons. First I must continue my race to the next aid station.

CHAPTER 8
FORESTHILL - MY PACER JOINS ME
(62.0 MILES)

Yet all experience is an arch where through
Gleams that untraveled world whose margin fades
Forever and forever when I move.
(Alfred Lord Tennyson)

I leave Michigan Bluff to the cheers and optimism of my crew, leaving my waist pack with them to have ready for me six miles later at Foresthill, when I will meet with my pacer, Rob. In my pack will be my prescription glasses for better night vision, my regular and small spare flashlight, and extra batteries. A couple of hours after Rob and I leave Foresthill it will become dark and we need to have good lights for the night portion of the race.

I gradually pick up speed and jog slowly but easily down a wide, gentle, dirt road away from the dust of the foot and car traffic at Michigan Bluff, eventually working out the soreness and stiffness from sitting for five minutes after many miles of running and walking. This is the only section of the course I have not run in practice so it becomes a new, small adventure. I come across a runner bent over standing in the middle of the road. He looks up and assures me that he is all right, that he just has some stomach problems and has thrown up. I feel sorry for him but he doesn't act worried, and there is nothing I can do to help him so I continue on, hoping it won't happen to me. I can only look out for myself at this point.

The road suddenly veers to the right off the main road. Yellow ribbons are splashed everywhere and lead to a short, steep climb. I seem to be going nowhere fast as I bend forward to push myself up the incline.

Looking behind me, I see no one is sight, and I suddenly feel like I'm the only one in the race, like I've been forgotten and abandoned; maybe I won't ever see anyone again. I encounter another one of those rare moments when the race seems to be non-existent. Suddenly I feel like a lost pioneer of a hundred years ago alone on the trail, seeking shelter and food. Civilization abruptly disappears like some science fiction movie. No one knows or cares where or why I am here; somehow I must move onward to somewhere out here in the wilderness. Here my soul is alone to seek out some direction in life, the way pointed out by a yellow ribbon tied to a tree branch and fluttering weakly in the warm breeze.

I continue slowly up the road as the sun begins radiating down its warmth on to my body. My fresh, dry shirt is already soaked with sticky sweat from the exertion. I pour a little water from one of my bottles on the top of my biking cap, letting it slowly seep through the soft material and down the side of my head, temporarily shocking my hot skin. I pour a few more precious drops on the back of my neck. The cooling respite is temporary but welcome. Within seconds the warmth is back seeking to burn my exposed skin.

I see the top of the hill and my body reaches out for it. I struggle with my thighs, pushing the knotting muscles to move me to the top. One last, short, gasping stride and I am ready to start the short, very steep climb down into Volcano Canyon, through the scrub brush and short trees, along a rutted-out path, difficult for balance and running downhill at the same time. The sun beats unmercifully on my body now and on the open, brown, dry dirt; the heat reflects doubly strong back into my face. I am about to enter one of the steepest and hottest sections of the entire run. Fortunately it is not as long as some of the other downhill portions of the trail.

My stomach abruptly and unexpectedly churns violently as I approach the beginning of my descent. I look about me and no one is present. Waves of nausea rare up suddenly and I bend over, letting it all go in a surge of embarrassing helplessness. Nothing comes out but I vomit three more times, until a weak trickle spews forth. Reluctantly and cautiously I lift my head, a pin-like chill penetrating the quiet heat of the sun and nipping at my skin. I glance around again and still no one is there; my own embarrassment is hidden among the trees and brush, the dirt and rocks. I breathe deeply, tentatively lift one leg and step forward, and then lifting the other, I begin to run again.

Oh, do I suddenly feel better! My bloated feeling is gone for the moment at least. For the initial time in several hours I can breathe easily as I start stumbling in a fractionally controlled trot down the chute of dusty trail, trying half successfully to lift my tired legs. I can't figure out why I don't stumble or fall with this style of running over such uneven terrain; maybe miles of constant repetition over the same type of terrain have put my legs on automatic. After my illness I discover with a sigh of relief that my mind is awake and my thoughts very alert and in focused clarity. My sickness provides me with a new kick of energy.

I begin to zero in now toward my next goal, Foresthill, and more importantly, joining my pacer. Being with my pacer is the one thought that uplifts me for the next few miles. It will loosen my mind to run with someone I have run with many times before, someone I know well who knows my physical and mental makeup. He is someone who is fresh himself both physically and mentally, someone whose energy I can draw off. It is a thought that is with me the rest of the way to Foresthill, my main driving force.

I begin to encounter several other runners; a couple pass me while I pass some of them. I finally reach the bottom of the dusty ravine and begin my walk up the steep, open, hot hill to the top of Volcano Canyon. I walk around a corner, my arms pumping when I encounter an ABC television crew with a camera and Diana Nyad, the marathon swimmer and commentator, standing in the middle of the road. Trying to look fresh and relaxed I ask her in the most friendly and unconcerned tone of voice I can muster at this moment if this is the way to Auburn. She laughs, taps me on the shoulder, and tells me that I'm over halfway there. She doesn't know really what a highlight of my day so far this is, enough to perk up my spirits and temporarily put my agonizing leg pains on hold.

The earlier runner I encountered who was bent over eventually catches up with me near the top of the canyon, and we continue our long walk up the hill together to Bath Road. He appears to be a friendly sort of person, and we engage in idle conversation, probably about the race, but I don't really remember. All I know is that our talking helps make time pass more quickly as we make our way to the top of the canyon.

We see the gate up ahead where the trail meets the beginning of Bath Road, which is only a short section to the highway now, and then less than a mile down the highway to Foresthill. I check the time on my watch, and we still remain on a good schedule. People appear everywhere along the road, waiting for their runners or just to give encouragement. Many people seem to know my new found running friend by name. Others seem to be totally disinterested in our progress, looking past us like we are invisible, probably waiting for friends to come up the hill, and also probably very tired from the many hours of endless waiting.

My friend and I stride with a relaxed pace up the pavement and can hear the traffic up ahead on the main road. It is a foreign sound, that of vehicles moving along a paved road, the whooshing of tires on asphalt, the dull drone of engines. It seems like I'm hearing it for the very first time in my life. Automobiles are a part of my everyday life, but I've never really heard them prior to this moment in quite this conscious manner. We reach the highway, turn left on the dirt path as the terrain levels out, and begin our journey down the Foresthill highway for less than a mile on the only part of the course that is really out in the center of civilization.

I suddenly feel naked and completely out of place running next to a highway, as if it were a 10K road race. People are parked along the side of the road and give us encouragement in a sort of low key way, while cars busily drive by like we aren't really present. I suddenly notice that I am hot and sweaty, my legs are covered with sticky, trail dust, and my shoes and socks are the colors of my legs, red and brown. I seem so incongruous to be slogging down next to a road at such a slow snail's pace, a pace which on the trail seems fast and comfortable.

I vaguely discern the checkpoint ahead becoming larger as I approach. I enter a sea of wall to wall people with blurry, cheering faces, and weave through the funnel until I find the scale. I jump quickly on the scale; despite the sickness and the heat, my weight is still all right, which is a good sign. The person weighing me releases me to my crew for a five minute rest, nourishment again, my pack already prepared for night running, and most of all the presence of my pacer, who is already to join me for the rest of the way.

My pacer, Rob Stephenson, is telling me enthusiastically how good I look and how he will get me through. The first thing that occurs to me is that he really doesn't know how I feel or what I have really gone through during the past 62 miles and 14 hours running and walking, of hoping, concentrating, and sometimes inwardly crying for relief from all of this. I try to appear fresh, but I know that I don't feel like I look. I do know that I could be worse off, that in my dreams, I had hoped to feel no worse than I do at this significant point in the race. My dream is still focused clearly as a smiling vision there in front of me to be had, and I know it. Rob can be the catalyst for me to achieve the reward of victory by the end of the night.

The individual who is allowed to run the last portion of the race with the official runner is called a pacer, yet his title doesn't really fit his real responsibilities. In the true sense of the word he doesn't really attempt to set a pace for his runner; that pace is already established by the runner after 60 plus miles of running. The true purpose and intent of a pacer is probably one of safety, since the runner has been out on the trail for endless hours and at this point is very fatigued; in addition, night is setting in and the runner's vision is reduced. A single tired runner carelessly moving at night who falls off an embankment might not be found for several days.

The author and his pacer Rob Stephenson just before the start of the race.

Having first run the Western States as a pacer, and about to experience the help of my own pacer as a contestant, I see him as an important link in the success or failure of trying to complete the 100 miles successfully. To the rest of the non-runners, the pacer is an anonymous entity, not really part of the race; to me he is a magnet, an important power to locate every ounce of strength for my soul in order to reach the finish line.

Rob is my pacer for this run and I choose him carefully from among my running friends. I could have chosen David, whom I had paced, but he moved to another city and wouldn't be available during training. I ask Rob if he would like to do it because I know we have compatible personalities,

I know he will be able to run with me all the way to the end, and finally, I know he wants to run the entire race some day and that this is a perfect experience in preparation for the run.

The months before the run, we take some solid runs together but we don't overdo it. Four key sessions stand out as milestones for the race. First we run the 16 mile new section of the trail together, that part we are now about to challenge, and he gets a first hand knowledge of that part of the trail. Next we run about 22 miles of trail in Sequoia National Park so we get used to working on trail-like terrain together. Third, we do one night run. We have some problems with our lights which we are able to work out, and we learn to adjust to the problems encountered while running together on a trail during the darkest hours of the night.

Finally we run a 50 mile race together, starting and finishing together, going at a slow, steady pace that is close to, although just a little faster than the 100 miler. The experience comes just four weeks before the Western States, and the fast recovery I experience and the strength I have at the end of the race, gives me solid confidence going into the big race. During many periods of these runs we talk a lot about many different running and non-running subjects and get to know each other just a little bit better than before.

My ideal pacer has certain personal qualities that will help me when I run. My pacer understands my running strengths and weaknesses. He knows I'm not blazing fast but at the same time knows I will keep going for a long time at a slow, steady pace. He understands me when I walk for awhile, that I am only attempting to recover and not because I'm ready to give up. He knows my comfort speed zone, senses if I'm going too slow, and will remind me to pick up the pace in a kindly manner. If I'm going a little faster than normal, he knows I'm feeling well and will let me go at that pace for awhile because he understands I'm locked into a comfortable rhythm.

My pacer does not dictate the pace; he will allow me to set my own pace. He learns my pace and will make sure I keep it up whether he is following or leading me. If I slacken too much, he will nudge me on. If he has to he will be firm with me, but if I'm doing well, he will encourage me to keep it up. If I'm feeling well and want to go faster, I'll tell him to lead me and go faster so I can pull on his strength, and he will know just how fast to go.

When I'm feeling lousy at some point along the lonely trail, he will listen patiently to and tolerate my gripes and complaints. I may continuously moan about every little pain in my body, every irritating little obstacle on the trail, and about every other topic that may have nothing whatsoever to do with running. He understands why I complain and becomes my sounding board, saying nothing or offering consolation whenever he feels it is possible to do so. When I am mentally down for a spell of time and expressing my feelings, he senses when to keep quiet and when to speak. If I complain about something he is doing, like setting too fast a pace, he understands I don't mean anything personal by it.

I give him special small, but important duties, like getting my bottles filled at aid stations. He makes certain that I eat some food when I am there, especially something salty. By this time I may not want any food, but he makes me take some in anyway. He checks to make sure I have taken care of all my needs at the aid stations and haven't left anything behind.

On the trail he asks me periodically if I have been drinking my fluids because the fatigue of running all day and night can cause me to forget to drink frequently when I may not be very thirsty. He reminds me occasionally about how far we have to go to the next checkpoint, what time it is, and how we are doing with the 24 hour pace. He lets me lead when I wish to but will take over the lead when I request it. If the trail ahead is unusually tough during the night, he will verbally guide me through the obstacles.

The personality of my pacer will be such that he knows that he has a difficult, maybe almost impossible job, yet at the same time, will not receive the glory he may richly deserve at the finish line. No one will know who he is at the end of the race as he disappears into the sea of spectators, and he takes quiet satisfaction in knowing that only his runner appreciates him. He works in the field of anonymity and he understands and completely accepts his quiet, crucial role. His only reward is seeing his runner win his race. There is no jealousy in his heart for he understands his role from the very beginning.

When my pacer takes off with me he has a race to run, a tough 38 mile trek, yet he is never a real finisher. He must run up and down tough hills on a trail that is often dangerous and full of obstacles, yet he gets no credit for running the race. He undergoes the same stresses as I do, expending energy to carry him twelve miles further than a marathon, yet he receives no award or official finishing time for his race. He has the added responsibility for my safety; he must have extra eyes, know first aid, be a good storyteller, have the strength of a mule, and finally, be a psychologist.

He must do all this and run those treacherous 38 miles at my pace, always adjusting his tempo to my tempo; he can stop only when I stop. Sometimes he must stop when he doesn't feel like stopping. He must walk when he doesn't feel like walking. He runs slowly when he would rather be running fast. My pacer must make sure my needs are constantly being met and at the same time encourage me to the finish line. In addition he must run his own race, and I don't ever bother to encourage him or make sure his needs are taken care of. A good pacer is an invaluable asset to the runner, and the runner really has no time during his race to worry about the welfare of his pacer. The pacer must be present at all times yet be an invisible but strong force out there in the darkening wilderness.

Pacing at the Western States is a difficult task. When the lights of the stadium and the finish line are finally in sight during the wee hours of a summer morning, the pacer quietly leaves the race and slinks into obscurity, melting in as part of the crowd, unknown to the lights and the cameras, the fame and glory. Only his runner really knows what he has done, and a little silent sign between racer and pacer allows the pacer to share in the glory. No matter what happens from this time forward a special bond is formed between the two that only they can comprehend.

As I stand up and prepare to leave after my five minute break, my crew leader tells me that I'm only minutes behind another runner we all know well, a sub-22 hour finisher from last year, who is having a bad day. He says we will catch him soon; I'll believe it when I see him.

The next section from the top of the canyon, the California Street Loop, a new 16 mile portion down to the Rucky Chucky River Crossing, might be the turning point in the race. If I can survive this seemingly easy, yet strangely difficult section of trail as darkness approaches, and arrive at the river crossing with some time to spare and with a spirit still remaining in my heart and legs, I feel I can make it to the finish line in under 24 hours.

I glance quickly at my watch and it reads almost seven o'clock, and the sun is beginning to descend toward the western horizon. Rob and I buckle up amid the cheers of our crew, and we take off for the short jog down the road in front of all the spectators and sea of humanity bustling about the town of Foresthill. Shortly we make a left hand turn and leave the town, disappearing once again back to the loneliness of the trail.

My race is on its most critical leg. The question is, will I survive it intact enough to be able to continue on?

As I continue along the trail of life, I find many of the critical aid stations along the way, those high points where certain milestones are reached. In my career as a teacher or coach it might be winning a championship or big game or presenting a critical lesson to my students where the light bulbs in their heads turn on brightly.

Just as Foresthill is the most civilized post along the course, certain events in my life tend to be more important than others. These are the precious moments when life really means something special. The other aid stations are also important, just as other life moments have significant meaning. Yet the gaining of a pacer and the concrete highway with real people may only for a moment bring back the normalcy of real life away from the trail. This moment becomes significant because it marks a critical point in the course, where the finish line finally becomes visible.

Life also has its aid stations along the way. But once in a while a Foresthill comes along, a life-altering event that marks some significant moment in life in which the finish of the race of life comes alive. Somehow I know when I have experienced such a milestone. From this moment on I know that life may be different in some way.

Yet as in the race, I must get back to the melodic beating of the trail, the seemingly endless monotonous plodding forward step by step to the next aid station. There is really no time to celebrate the significant events in life, for the journey must pick up where it left off and continue on down the wild trail of life. I may be changed in some way, but I must continue on and put any type of celebration off until much later, only when I have reached the real finish line. Life is like that; time continues to march forward with nothing in its way to keep it from the final finish line.

CHAPTER 9
JOURNEY DOWN TO RUCKY CHUCKY
(78.0 MILES)

Only those who will risk going too
far can possibly find out how far they
can go. Those who dare to dream, dare
to do ....

(Saying)

I leave the town of Foresthill with my pacer Rob to enter into the 16 miles of no return, 16 miles into the canyon to the river crossing, miles of easy descent, but mile after mile of erratic plunging.

I encounter a winding trail with many short up and down fragments, many steeps both ways, reducing me often to walking and sliding even on the downhills. I approach the darkness of the night, and I will meet him before I get to the bottom of this mountainside. Already the shadows begin to envelop the chasm of the narrow canyon. I approach that 65 mile plus point at some point on the trail, beyond which I have never traveled before, and the occurrence vaguely registers before my mind. Somewhere along the line of racing new distances, I have always had to pass new, uncharted distances so this mark becomes only an individual symbol for yet another milestone achieved.

Most urgent to the success of my race, I will approach a gigantic moment of truth by the time I arrive at the 78 mile point that crosses the river, a moment that goes beyond mere fatigue, beyond the normal physical and mental stress my body and mind must endure. It is here on this section that many will succumb, will call it enough, and wait for another year.

By the time I reach the depth of the abyss my fate in this race may be secured and that thought alone threatens my mental concentration. I must block it out and continue solidly and methodically on the path, one step at a time, forcing my mind to tell my body that I only pursue attaining the river, 16 miles away. This is my race now, 16 miles long to the river crossing, and every part of the run before or beyond is only a distant memory.

My big advantage is that I now have company, my pacer and friend, who is fresh in body and spirit, who helps pull me along in my ordeal, encouraging me all the rest of my pilgrimage. We run briefly on the streets of Foresthill, past the throngs of spectators and bystanders, suddenly turning left down a street; we cross another road and head out alone as one entity to the far canyon below us.

The author's crew members Bob Kearney and Len Hansen, the author, Roger Sebert, Roger's crewmembers Louie Martin and Larry Nava near the starting line the day before the race.

The first couple of miles is renewing time. We talk about what has happened to us during the day. I tell him about my race so far and try to convey to him how I feel, despite the inadequacy of the attempt. I try to run with enough surge to show him that I am doing well, but I don't know whether or not he thinks I am going very fast at all. After all he is rested and fresh from a full day of relaxation and preparation. At this point a surge of speed to me is to him really nothing more than a slow jog. Speed is only relative to each of us according to how we feel.

Rob tells me about his day so far, but I also know he is feeling me out, checking carefully without asking to see how strong I am so he will comprehend how hard and how much he can push me. We both know there are only a limited number of subjects we can pursue at this point, and I would prefer that he do most of the talking, the effort to speak too often subtly expending minute reserves of surviving energy.

The early conversation is excellent revival therapy, and so far we run downhill, some terrain gentle and some fairly steep. I am aware gradually of creeping shadows as the sun slowly edges toward the western horizon. We run toward the dipping sun, but as we begin to shift back and forth across the mountainside, the sun's orb and its warmth darts in and out from behind the mound of hillsides on the twisting trail. One big plus for the coming nighttime hours is that the sun won't be beating its heat down on our bodies any longer.

I take the lead and run ahead of Rob for the moment as we pad down the trail. The clock moves slowly as we move, or at least it appears to. We begin walking occasionally on some uphill and level sections. The trail heads down into the canyon, but it starts making irritating detours back up the flanks of small slopes. I can see where we will eventually end up, which is a long way to the bottom of the canyon, but we never seem to move downward. We wind around the hill; then we go up and back down again. Finally we encounter a small aid station in the middle of nowhere. From somewhere a couple of vehicles find this spot, and several people are here to offer help to the runners. We stoke up on water, I stuff down a couple of salty food items, and we continue on with barely a pause.

My crew chief has mentioned that we are only minutes behind a fellow runner we know, a good runner who ran a great race the previous year, finishing in the top 30. Suddenly slightly below and ahead of us on a switchback we see him and his pacer, another friend of ours. I can sense he is struggling for some reason, and we quickly make up ground on him. They step aside to let us pass them, and we exchange greetings with each other and then continue on again. I feel energized slightly, knowing I have passed this exceptional runner. Aching power temporarily surges through my legs, pushing me forward rhythmically downward further to the river.

I go up a short hill now at a walk with Rob following. This is about the fourth hill during the last 15 minutes, and I start talking out loud to myself, asking when the downhills are going to begin and continue permanently for awhile. We reach the top, the trail suddenly dropping off sharply for a couple of hundred yards, making running almost impossible. My thighs burn intensely as I slide and brake down the bank, dust flying as we skid and try to keep from stumbling over small rocks.

Falling is on my mind as I proceed gingerly down the embankment. A rock kicks loose and rolls with me. Other small rocks are hidden under the thick dust, waiting to trip me. The stirred dust puffs into my eyes, blurring my vision slightly in the dimming shadows. I slip slightly, almost losing my balance as my shoe slides over the loose stones. I can hear Rob behind me having the same problems all the while talking to himself. I curse to myself because I expect to make up time going downhill after walking the uphills, but I must slow down because of the steepness of the downhill.

The skies get darker now, and we are thinking of pulling out our flashlights, but they won't take effect for quite awhile yet. We exchange positions with several other runners and their pacers and continue on, the sun no longer shining on us, the darkening shadows instead getting blacker and commencing to envelop us on the mountainside. My recently passed running friend catches back up and passes me, apparently renewed again. They ask me if I know how much cushion we have on a 24 hour pace, and I tell them I think about 30 or 40 minutes. At least, I know this is the cushion I had at Foresthill, and from the relative ease and patience I've gone from there so far, I figure it is about the same.

I continue running the rolling trail, usually with a few more downs, but the steepness of the downhills is really aggravating my quads, jabbing jolts of pain through them as I brake and skid. I grit my teeth, trying to ignore the pain, attempting to make believe it really isn't present. We repass our friend again, and this time I don't realize it, but we will not see him anymore; he will drop out at the river crossing.

As the day continues to darken into night I curse even louder that we aren't making progress, that we just keep running what seems like the same section of trail while constantly shifting gears. We don't seem to be getting anywhere at all. I am now getting frustrated having to walk all the uphills, and I can almost hear the clock ticking loudly and speeding up. Rob takes the lead for awhile, and he tells me to travel sideways down the steep sections to relieve the pain.

Out of desperation I try it, following his example as he hops down the bank fighting for balance. We stir the dust and kick loose rocks that follow us down the bank. Our speed is slow but faster than walking, and the pain is much less. I try two different ways, alternating techniques every minute or so. I turn my body to the right and take short steps, crossing my right leg over my left. Next I simply shuffle my right foot down to my left foot and plant it next to and above my left foot without crossing over steps. I then take a big step sideways with my left foot and repeat the sequence.

The first system is faster, but I alternate techniques to give me relief from aches by varying the use of muscle groups. I am also aware of avoiding jamming my toes against the ends of my shoes. My shoes are laced firmly and tied off tightly to prevent slippage. The triangular studs on the bottoms sometimes slip but also clasp firmly on a surface which is somewhat like thick ice-covered marbles.

Darkness is descending now like a huge theater curtain dropping down to the stage. I put my glasses on for better vision. My slightly blurred vision in daylight hours becomes amplified doubly in the impending darkness. My prescription glasses bring those hazy outlines back into vivid focus during the night. Now only the night and not my eyes can alter my sight.

The flashlight really doesn't take effect yet, but without it I can't see as well as in the lighted daylight hours. I must concentrate more carefully, tilting my head downward to place my eyes closer to the trail to better see the changing texture of the darkening dirt, twigs, roots, and rocks.

The slowly disappearing light plays tricks on my vision. In the open areas of the trail with no trees, adequate light is present to help me make out the contour of the trail. Then suddenly I plunge into a section where tall trees grow on either side of me. They cast dark shadows on the already sunless and shadowless trail. The sudden blackness from these trees makes seeing with distinction difficult on the trail ahead.

I turn on my light for the first time, but it only vaguely outlines the trail to help me distinguish obstacles. The rays barely penetrate the half light, half blackness, the shadowy descending twilight. Suddenly I stagger out of the shadows and into the open again, and the flashlight is now totally useless in the quickly emerging semi-brightness.

The moment of time between when the sun sets and true darkness settles in seems to take forever. Observing the creeping fingers crawl toward total darkness is like watching the hour hand on a clock, unable to see it moving, but knowing intellectually it is creeping along like a snail crossing a road. Darkness is becoming complete, but I can't see the event actually occurring. Once the blackness is secure around me, enveloping me totally, then my light will remain on and effective for the many long hours before the sun rises in the eastern sky.

Rob and I continue on with him in the lead; he constantly encourages me and leads me in our slides down the steeps. In some places the trail begins to mold itself into some gradual downhill sections, and I gingerly try to stride out, my stiffening muscles stretching out with crying, tearful objection to keep up with Rob's long, loping strides. I suddenly realize that I haven't turned my light off for quite some time. I notice only a simmering fading light in the horizon and understand that the real night has enveloped us completely in its grasp to take us hopefully all the way to the finish line.

We are in total darkness when we reach the second aid station on the California Loop. Quickly we get what we need, thank the personnel, and head on out. Several runners are resting here, seated in lawn chairs and lying on cots, in another spot of remoteness out on a very isolated section of the course. These small aid stations on this 16 mile section have obviously had to work diligently at getting their supplies and people into these secluded points. As we continue on, Rob fights a problem he has throughout the night, his waist pack bouncing up and down on his hips; he has difficulty securing it tightly. It doesn't help that he has somewhat of a bouncy stride anyway. At some point he reaches back and discovers that he has left a pocket open and a couple of flashlight batteries have fallen out and are lost.

Another sound now slowly penetrates my senses. The quiet of the woods, the occasional chirp of a bird, is now invaded by the subtle and fresh whoosh of the river just below us in the canyon. We are now close to the bottom of the canyon, but we can't see it in the total darkness; we can only judge by our ears, as the flowing waters tell us in their unique language and music that we are on a course of destiny to meet them somewhere in the darkness. My mind envisions the familiar course of a river rushing downward over rocks, settling in a quiet, deep pool of hidden treasures, and picking up speed at the shallowing of the pool to rush again over the rocks. I have lived on a river and I see it all, hiding beneath me in the nighttime, holding inside its secret riches but revealing its presence to me by the only thing it can't hide, the gentleness of its steady, melodic, calling voice.

The darkness, the strange projection of our lights whipping back and forth over the trail, and the unchanging sound of the water hundreds of feet directly below us, distracts my thoughts away from the agonizing, burning pain in my legs. I begin to feel almost detached from the blackened, godly presence surrounding me, from the race itself; it becomes a surreal adventure, a movement into an area almost non-earthly, non-physical. The new joyous sounds envelop my new consciousness.

We pitch downward and finally enter the final aid station on this loop. Only about three more miles are left to go to the river crossing. The sound of the rushing water remains close by; we can almost reach out and touch the river, but we can't see it. Aid personnel tell us we have one more hill to go up; this doesn't seem possible at this point, but they are correct when we discover we shortly must climb up a short, steep section of dirt road. The pitch is very abrupt. I search out the deep recesses of my memory but can't remember this hill in my practice run.

Finally we proceed down near the river itself. My feet now run in soft beach sand, both feet skidding to the side out of control with each plant, with no solid base from which to push off. I feel like I'm reliving a nighttime dream where I'm being pursued but can't seem to make any progress in escaping. An overgrown stream branch just misses my head as I duck, and it slaps against my shoulder. I hear sand flying as Rob spins his own legs ahead of me; we are now level with the river, climbing short dirt banks before heading back to sand again. The rushing water is now intimate; I feel I can reach out and touch it. Each individual drop seems to call out its own unique octave as it plunges over another smooth stone.

I remember to start drinking the rest of my water from my bottles as we inch closer to the river crossing. Finally on a high point above the river, the trail suddenly turns toward an old road and levels off; running is easier now. I lift my head and see a weak glow ahead of me bouncing off the rocky canyon cliffs. I lumber along for a few more minutes and look again, acutely aware that the lights are the glow from the river crossing only a mile or so ahead.

From now on to the crossing the lights become our guide, as we slowly move closer with each measured, painful step. I check my watch and it is about 10:30, almost three and a half hours since we started from the top of the canyon. Another 10 minutes will bring us to perhaps the key moment in my race. I notice that my body generally feels all right, although I don't know what I should feel like, never having gone this far before. My legs ache but not any more than they did 16 miles ago. My stomach is very settled and feels empty. I have gone nearly 78 miles, 13 miles further than I've ever gone before, a thought that occurred to me at Foresthill, but I realize I've been so involved in moving forward and taking in the mystery of the course and the new, night darkness, that I haven't thought about it again until now.

Well, I think, we are almost here, the one section of the course that people will always talk about, the river crossing. It's now time to see how I'll get through it, but first I must encounter the aid station, a weigh-in, and my tired crew members who have worked hard this time to be prepared to meet me here.

As I look back at the race, I realize that life's little adventures are much like the trek down to Rucky Chucky. First of all, I reach a point on the trail in distance beyond which I have never traveled before. In life we have new challenges that we face that we are never totally sure that we can conquer, but we continue on and try anyway, just I pass that invisible line beyond 62 miles, the most miles I had ever done before non-stop. It feels strange but I plunge onward toward the unknown anyway with the knowledge that I had prepared myself the best I could, just as in life.

The trail becomes a frustrating series of small ups and downs. Just when the trail seems to smooth out, out pops up another difficult section. We have those same ups and downs in life, moments when euphoria hits us as we meet some unexpected success; then we experience those temporary lows when we meet failures that we don't expect, especially those little difficulties where we depend on the incompetence of someone else to get us through. But through the temporary depressions of spirit we make it through anyway and things finally come out all right. Just as we do out on the trail, we must exert patience in the face of adversity because we know we can persevere until things are right again.

On this section of the trail, darkness slowly sets in as my pacer and I plunge down toward the river crossing. Nighttime seems scary to most people, especially out in the woods. It is easy to become lost and disoriented, and we wonder what evils lurk in the night. In fact, black

86

often is a symbol of evil. Yet as a runner I learn to embrace the night because the air cools and there becomes a certain inner peace in running in the darkness. I can be alone and far away from the scrutiny of people on the course. Often in life when trouble begins to creep upon us, we too can relax and embrace the darkness of life and use it to concentrate and turn it to a positive factor to get us out of trouble.

When my trail of life suddenly becomes frustrating with irritants, I take a deep breath, laugh at the situation, because soon my trail will smooth out once again and the sun will rise in the east.

CHAPTER 10
RIVER CROSSING - DRAMA UNFOLDS

If it weren't for the rocks in its bed,
the stream would have no song.
(Saying)

The most dramatic segment of this race is crossing the river at night. Rob and I behold the reflections of gigantic floodlights bouncing off canyon walls back into the eerie darkness. We view this odd, white kaleidoscope coming from around the corner of a precipice as we pad along in the dark on the jeep road flowing above and parallel to the river. The rushing, symphonic music of the river below my feet warns me how tight I am to the fast moving, swirling water.

We advance onward like soldiers for a few minutes before I glance up again to see the lights approaching nearer and nearer, their bright, ghostly arcs now totally visible to my eyes and no longer just reflections off the rocks. We can hear and even sense frantic activity on both sides of the river as we slowly and gingerly pick our way over a couple of detours where the dirt road has been washed out by an old, gigantic slide. The hum of generators for the lights slowly penetrates our ears, and voices become very distinct in the blackness, no longer half-imagined sounds mixed in with the breezes playing in the trees. My worry about making it in a decent time is past as I instinctively realize that we are still on a fairly consistent time schedule, perhaps a little slower than I anticipated, but not by very much.

My legs begin to recover from the torturous, treacherous hills and relax again by gliding through the easy and level terrain. An invisible force pulls them along strongly, perhaps aided by the fact that I will see my crew again. My mind looks forward to enjoying the short respite I will find here, the center of attention in one of the most intoxicating places on the course. Without notice or warning we stumble suddenly out of the dark, night air into the flood lit arena of the aid station, with robot-like people sitting stiffly and unmoving in chairs as mysterious apparitions in the deep shadows, someone asking us to call out our numbers.

I take off my pack and quickly bound on the scale. The attendant slips the balancing mechanism back and forth until it finally settles right on my starting weight, and when some blank human form asks me how I feel, I definitely don't feel I am lying when I comment coolly that I feel pretty well; at least mentally I know I am at a high point. I have managed to survive the raw, extended, and also difficult previous section in relatively good shape, and I clearly know that I have 22 miles to go; for the first time I see the silver gate in my inner vision waiting for me at the end of my encounter.

My crew sits me down, props me up, and tends to my needs, which consists of a quick massage and some hot soup provided by the aid station; almost steamy hot liquid slides easily down my throat, spreading tingles of deep warmth throughout my insides. I taste a smattering of salt but can't identify the solid substance in the liquid. One crew member fills my bottles, this time with a half and half

The author paces runner Edwin Demoney across the river during the 1987 race.

mixture of water and Max. My change of shoes and socks are in my drop bag across the river, so I don't really need anything else at this point. However, the friendly but tired banter of familiar voices on shadowy faces and genuine words of encouragement pick me up mentally even more for the difficult section ahead.

I look around me and am amazed at the beehive of activity. The scene before me gives off an atmosphere of being on some foreign planet or some strange alien soil. Ghost-like people are moving, talking, and shouting indistinct sounds above the steady roar of the river and the moan of the generators. Shadows cast eerily across the tents and rocks as bodies move in strange, distorted angles across the bright floodlights. All forms have no form; everything is hazy and outlined in shadows, a strange mask play being performed before a raptured audience of one. Faces become focused only when they are inches away from each other. For a moment the whole scene takes my mind off my own suffering and anguish.

Rob and I finally rise and take off from our moment of respite and after asking for directions, head for the crossing point of the river. I take the lead and enter a rocky drop off of large, awkwardly leaning boulders down to the river. The bright floodlights make the setting even brighter than it would be during the daylight hours, but slightly out of focus. I slowly pick my way down and around the huge boulders, slipping lightly in sand, seeing human figures on both sides of the river waiting for us. I remember two people here in the shadows, one I believe a black woman seated in a chair taking down our numbers perhaps, another a man with a big flashlight who speaks to us. He firmly directs us to the left around a boulder and out of the glare of the spotlight. He tells us to step where he shines his flashlight. I focus more clearly as I step out of the direct glare of the giant, stage lights.

While cautiously picking my way with my eyes cast downward, I am suddenly aware that I am standing in shallow water half way up the sides of my shoes. I look up, and the huge rope looms before me and I grab it firmly with one hand. The rope jiggles slightly, its own weight preventing it from being stretched tightly. I step down into the deep, cold, slowly moving water, ready for the shock. At first I feel nothing as the icy water envelops my shoes and socks. With the water finally soaking through, abruptly the cold hits me, similar to the shock of diving into an ice cold swimming pool. It is really not different from all the years I have spent wading while fly fishing, that sudden coldness of the river water on my feet and legs when first submerging them.

The entire canyon is lit up brightly, with the river the stage; I am the star on that stage. It is my moment in the spotlight. Looking up I am blinded by the painful glare. I'm only aware of shadows on the other side of the river where the lights originate. Behind me Rob stumbles a little trying to get his footing, and I tell him he will have to put his flashlight in his pack so he can use two hands on the rope. He has no room to put it in, so he awkwardly stuffs it in his shirt which is wrapped around his waist. The fool is still wearing no shirt.

Every 15 or 20 feet along the rope someone stands in the cold water, almost waist deep, facing upstream to guide us verbally across the river. In the daytime, this section would be a gently flowing and relatively shallow wide section of the river. At night under the bright lights, it seems like a rushing madhouse of self-consuming water desperate to make its way downstream.

The guides tell us where the rocks are located, but the bright lights shine down so intensely and directly on the water that I can focus distinctly on every boulder under the water; each little uneven surface on every rock stands out and glares back to me magnified by the lense of the water surface. One guide tells me the way has been built up with boulders, that I should try to follow them so I won't sink too deeply into the water. That water is over my knees as I move forward.

I lunge slightly off balance to the next rock in a couple of spots, but the movement is easy, especially with the heavy rope to hang on to. I will myself not to look upstream at the water rushing toward me; I have that inner fear of walking along the edge of a cliff. One false step will propel me headlong downstream. I know my fears are exaggerated, but I can't help myself. I clutch tightly with both hands, ready to squeeze down like a clamp if I should suddenly slip. Slowly we pick our way across the rushing stream one slow, clock-moving step at a time. The water rushes along now smoothly with barely a sound, for there are no rocks sticking their heads above the deep, pool-like surface to divert the liquid and send it into its eternal music. I can hear that music faintly pushing upstream from the rapids just below me as the water picks up speed and topples across more stones and boulders.

I see no other runners ahead of me, and I didn't see any right behind us when we entered the water. Could it be that we are the only ones in the river at this moment? Mysteriously when we reach the other side a few other runners seem to appear, or are they just aid station personnel? It's difficult to tell in this moonlike scene.

As I near the middle of the stream I decide that humor is in order so I ask the guide across from me if the fishing is any good, and he laughs back quietly and says something unintelligible. It is strange now that despite the bright lights, I can't remember what one face looks like or how many people are actually standing in the river to guide me across. I do distinctly remember thanking one of them for being crazy enough to stand out there in the cold water for all that time. I'm sure he really knows who the crazy one is.

The cold actually refreshes my tired legs, and I experience no cramps at all. Finally the water becomes shallow and I gingerly and quickly step on a rock and finally plant my feet on a solid bank, the icy water dripping from my legs and shoes, the cool, night air splashing against my bare skin. One of the aid personnel on the other side asks if I have cramps and I explicitly recall how well I feel. I do, however, experience a little overall body chill after leaving the water. My shirt is wet from perspiration and I shiver a little bit, but I have a windbreaker in my drop bag to warm me. I notice that the aid personnel seem laid back over here on the other side, almost nonchalant. They seem to ignore me, and their eyes are focused out on the river and the center stage. My drop bag is waiting for me as I clamber up the bank to the flat portion where the simple crude station is set up. One nice gentleman has obviously been assigned just to me; he helps me change my shoes and socks and get some more warm soup to settle the chill. As I sit in a lawn chair, time seems distant to me. Hours have passed since I arrived on the opposite side, or so it seems. My race is going too slowly to make it to the finish line before the sun rises.

I put on my windbreaker without zipping it up and reattach my waist belt. With dry shoes and socks my feet feel snug and warm, and I am ready for the long, tedious climb out of the canyon. I am surprised as I look at my watch that it takes about 15 minutes from the time I first reach the aid station on the opposite bank to this moment; though not very much time has passed, it is still much too long, I think. It is a few minutes before 11 o'clock; however, I am still on schedule, six hours to do 22 miles. The time spent here is probably money in the bank as Rob and I set out for our final journey to Auburn.

Bundled up and dry, I begin the walk up the hill, Rob right beside me. I look over and the crazy fool still hasn't put on his shirt. This sucker is tough, I think, and off we go together, chattering, our flashlights reflecting crazily off the dirt road ahead of us.

The River sings in all its infinite wisdom. When it is angry it roars its displeasure over the giant boulders that are strewn in its pathway. When it is happy it plays a gentle waltz across the smooth sands and small pebbles that stroke its ego on the quiet, gradual downhill flow. The River is smart; it has a plan of attack in its life and follows that plan to its completion. It twists and turns but it stays on its path in an unending fashion, rarely casting its path in another direction. Yet even with this plotted path, the River is free in spirit and energy and it is never afraid to vary its experiences or to take on new challenges. No two parts of the river are the same. Each pool, each configuration of rocks, each little eddy and riffle is unique.

The River follows the path of its life's journey, yet is free to be unique along the journey itself. Could we all do much better than to emulate the River?

As I sit on a rock along a free flowing river 20 years after my journey on the trail, I listen closely to what it has to say. The river seems the same as it was 20 years ago, yet I know that it too has changed in many subtle ways just as I have changed. Over the many years, storms and high waters have altered the banks and the boulders; the various pools are not exactly the same configuration as they were 20 years ago. The river has matured just as I have. It has gotten older just I have. Its strength is still present but in perhaps different ways, just as mine are. It still sings its one note tune, but perhaps in a slightly different key, just as my own tune is different from 20 years ago.

Although I can't run like I use to and have slowed down physically, I am much like the river, for I have just adjusted the way I do things in life, still enjoying each activity and movement, only in new and different ways. As I watch the stream drop gently down its bed, I live in this special moment and enjoy it for this special moment will never happen again at any time and in the same way. Although the river appears to be the same as always, each drop of water that flows across the rocks is unique, providing its unique moment on the canvas of the stream.

As I wade across the river while fly fishing 20 years after my trail journey, I remember back when I once crossed the river in a unique journey that will forever remain with my psyche.

CHAPTER 11
AUBURN LAKES TRAIL - KEEP MOVING
(85.2 MILES)

Sail forth-steer for the deep water only,
Reckless O Soul, exploring, I with thee, and thou with me,
For we are bound where mariner has not yet dared to go,
And we will risk the ship, ourselves and all.
(Walt Whitman)

The walk up the hill on a nice smooth road is easy and relaxing but not exactly a way I envision to make up time after all the progress lost in getting across the river and taking two breaks back to back. Leaving the excitement of the drama behind creates a temporary letdown as the only thing ahead is the obscurity of darkness. It is just before 11 o'clock in the evening.

Yet my hopes immediately pick up as I realize I am now on the last lengthy section before the end of the race, and soon the reflections of the finish line will creep into my mind. When I set out down toward the river I knew that section would be critical to my success. Suddenly I realize that I have made it to the river and across the rushing torrent, and here I am continuing on, not only on schedule time-wise, but feeling reasonably vigorous as well.

The stretch ahead to the highway is about 15 miles of good trail, including many long segments of level running, ideal for weary legs. It is in part a long, excruciatingly boring section that seems to go on unceasingly without end. Yet this fact alone makes it welcome to the footsore, fatiguing runner. I have few concerns to worry about now; my only anxiety is that I just keep moving forward, plugging along slowly and patiently, knowing that some time in the hours ahead I will reach the end.

I run with my light jacket on over my T-shirt to cut down the chill of the river crossing. As I advance along the course, imperceptibly gaining mile after agonizing mile, I warm up and no longer feel the chill, but I keep the jacket on anyway, still not zipped but held together by the tightness of my waist pack. I am afraid if I take it off, the cool morning air will meet the wet perspiration of my T-shirt and chill me further. I can't afford to let my body temperature get lower. Sudden shivering might cause me to lose control of my delicately balanced pace.

I become a little warm at times but the warmth and the sweat feel like friends, keeping my blood circulating, allowing my muscles to relax and function like one single machine, and permitting my mind to remain alert. I never take the jacket off, except to change shirts once at an aid station. Rob runs shirtless all the way during our run together. We certainly must look like a strange pair, one clad in bare skin and one in a windbreaker proceeding methodically along the narrow trail.

We walk up the hill toward the Green Gate, a small aid station just under two miles away, set up just prior to the trail leveling off for a long run along the side of a canyon. Rob worries that we are going too slowly, too conservatively, that we are losing time, but I know it's useless to be concerned at this point. Since I am rested I try running part of this section, but my spirits are short lived by minor muscle cramping, throbbing quads, and I walk again but at a hasty clip. The pain remains but not as violently as when I run. I can endure the ebb of the piercing discomfort to the one of greater intensity.

Little green flare or glow sticks as well as yellow ribbons are positioned along the road every hundred yards. We see these flares the rest of the race, a new feature for the night portion of the race. The green glow is very small but can be seen at a long range by the naked eye. At first the stick looks a long distance away, but as we walk toward it, suddenly we are right beside it. Because the light is so tiny yet radiates so powerfully, it appears to me as being far off. I stare at it and it seems to come alive and darts at odd angles. When I realize the nearness of the glow, the vertigo of the dark and my distorted depth perception almost causes me to stumble. It is the sensation of thinking the bottom step is there and dropping down the foot quickly only to suddenly meet the rising floor.

We walk side by side, our flashlights playing out their arcs across the road, picking up the ruts and holes, stones and small dirt mounds on the beaten path. We talk about the activities of the river crossing. My feet, which at one time coming down the California Loop felt tired and sore under the base of my toes, feel warm and secure encased in both fresh, white socks and clean, dry shoes. The throbbing in my thighs is still present, but it seems just like a natural part of my being, something I must bear to the finish. Each uphill step vibrates the suffering slightly, waking it up momentarily to my consciousness, and I feel weakness as I push off each step.

I look back down into the canyon as we walk upward and see the faint glow of lights from the canyon like a soft, distant radiance from some remote spaceship. We have wound around the hillside so much that I lose my sense of direction and think the lights should be coming from another direction. Momentarily I don't understand why the lights come from the direction I see them, although I know it can't be a mistake. We are up so high on the mountainside now that the sound of the river is gone, and we are moving quietly along with the night sounds as we continue our trek. The only disturbance is the appearance of an occasional runner and his pacer walking more slowly than us or overtaking us from behind.

Just as the walk seems to go on without ending, we see the faint lights up ahead of the checkpoint on the road. We hear people talking and moving about. We approach them walking slowly and check in. Rob grabs a cup of coke and downs it quickly. I really don't need anything but top off my bottles before continuing onward. We check out and walk over to a split in the trail.

The road continues upward but the trail for the race splits to the right, beginning a long circuit of relatively level running, with only a few gently rolling up and down segments. We pan our lights back and forth like beams from a lighthouse, picking out globs of yellow ribbons leading us on the correct trail. It is so close to the aid station that the people here won't let us get lost. I can feel them watching us to make sure we take the correct route.

We start running the five miles plus to Auburn Lakes Trail, the next major station where my weight will be taken once again. The trail meanders along now with a few small obstacles but generally without any major obstructions. It proceeds in a velvety, rolling manner with frequent, gradual variations of upward and downward tilts like a small roller coaster. I still walk on the uphills but I try to run as much as possible when I can muster up enough energy to prime my muscles into a running motion. Rob leads and I follow about 10 to 15 feet behind to avoid kicking obstacles that I might approach too quickly if I'm too close to him.

Looking ahead, I see another pair of lights bobbing up and down ahead and to our right. From these lights I can see that the trail is winding around the side of a mountain, dipping back into gullies and going back out to ridge points. We quickly gain ground and catch and pass a runner and his pacer with a short, muffled exchange of greetings.

I notice my light is getting a little dim, although it still gives out enough light to pick out the trail if I squint a little. Rob's light is much brighter than mine so I figure my batteries are getting weak. They have lasted since it first became dark, way back halfway down the California Loop. We stop on a wide point of the trail; I quickly reach for fresh batteries without seeing what I am doing, putting the old ones back in one of my pack pockets. I flip on the switch, hear a small, brief popping noise, and my light fails to come on. I shake the flashlight, recheck the battery alignment, and put it back together. It still doesn't work, and I realize the bulb has burned out.

The two runners we have just passed re-pass us as I fiddle with my light, tapping and shaking it to try to get it working again. In every aspect I have over planned for the race, and lights are no exception. I reach down and pull my small, but fairly powerful, spare light off my waist pack where I have clipped it on and rotate the head. A steady, medium beam slices out into the darkness, but I worry because I have only one set of spare batteries, and in the past the small batteries sometimes go dead quickly with this particular light. Rob tells me that if we can make it to the highway, our crew will have another flashlight for me. I know I can probably make it that far with this light. Later on after the race, I wonder why I just didn't carry a spare bulb with me; this is the first time in my life I have ever had a flashlight bulb burn out on me.

Rob stuffs the useless flashlight into my pack and zips it up. We take off again, Rob still in the lead. The short rest and the standing during the light problem seems to pick up the energy in my legs, and I feel like I am going to be able to run for quite awhile. Inadvertently my problem has given me a chance to recover some energy, helping my battered legs to sop up some new strength.

We now become aware of the time element. It is well after midnight, and the dark is punctuated by the night sounds, the rasping crickets in tune with the air temperature, the rustles in the black bushes of unknown nighttime inhabitants. Rob and I make our own sounds, the scraping of our studded shoes against the trail, the jouncing, muffled racket of our waist packs bouncing up and down with each stride, the occasional cough and gut-uttered sound. We talk occasionally but keep moving, hoping to see a light ahead announcing the next aid station.

MOONEY GROVE PARK

VISALIA CALIFORNIA

The End of the Trail statue in Visalia, California.

We run for what seems forever. We round a corner to more darkness, continuing our easy shuffle. We go up a short incline and reduce our strides to a walk. Down the other side of the gentle slope and back to level pathway we go. The trail doesn't seem to end; around another corner we go and encounter more darkness, more deep blackness. I sip and then rapidly drink water from my plastic bottle, gulping it down. The invisible clock in my head ticks louder and louder as we approach the up side of one o'clock, just over four hours to go before the alarm goes off with its brash ringing announcing the time deadline. The winner has long crossed the finish line by now and is probably asleep.

On we go around another corner. We see two lights ahead, but they belong only to another runner and his pacer. No aid station is in view yet. The miles seem like ten; maybe someone measured it wrong. When will we get there? I drink more water, the taste no longer just bland but gone and uncomfortable. I hate the non-taste of the clear liquid. I'm not thirsty but I need it to pour into my body. My jacket is still half-unzipped and my shirt is damp with cold sweat. The air feels summer frigid, and if I take the jacket off, I fear I will get chills when the nippy breeze contacts the damp shirt stuck to my bare skin. I leave the jacket on. I reach my fingers inside the lenses of my glasses and half wipe away and half smear a slight fog of perspiration from around the edges. Everything on me and about me seems alive, on edge, and uncomfortable, but I continue with one foot plant at a time, remembering to be patient.

Rob says he hears something, and sure enough I hear the sound moments later, a deep, throaty rumble puncturing the black, night air. It is a generator, the generator that operates the lights for the next checkpoint. I gulp more water; I must keep my weight up. I should be hungry by now, but just the thought of food revolts my stomach.

We round a corner and the glow of a faint light reflects its beams off the trees and bushes below and to the right. The generator drones like some injured monster of the woods, but the single tone is a welcome relief to our exhausted, stumbling bodies. The trees are outlined in the light as we approach still running, their shadows shifting constantly as our eyes take a new point of view with each stride. I tell Rob there is a downhill to the checkpoint, remembering my pacing from last year. The station is set quite a distance below us, off a steep, dirt bank. Suddenly the trail switchbacks sharply and quickly like an S, pitching straight down off the bank. The switchbacks abruptly stop and we start sliding down a dirt bank like two lost madmen who suddenly discover their long, lost campground. Rob curses as he goes ahead of me, his feet almost slipping out from under him. I hesitate a moment before sliding so I'm not too close to him; I then step outward and plunge down after him.

We hit the bottom of the quick, short drop-off and are now level with the checkpoint. We walk vigorously across a flat spot of smooth ground to the check in area. I glance at my watch which indicates about ten minutes before one o'clock. We have just over four hours to complete just under 15 miles. We are right on schedule still, but I don't feel totally comfortable with our margin. I temporarily envision myself sprinting to make it under 24 hours but immediately block out the thought.

The first item to check is my weight, and, thank goodness, it is exactly on my starting weight. Ghostly, dark aid personnel ask how I feel. The shadows and darkness and the bright lights mix in to create hazy features on faces, individual people becoming so much as one clone, all faces as one. I receive some hot soup and sit in a chair for a few minutes as Rob brings the drop bag over.

I make only one change here. In the cool night air, I strip my jacket off and quickly remove my wet shirt. My skin feels comfortable as I replace the damp shirt with a dry one with words on it that I have saved for the finish line, if I reach it. I decide to replace my jacket so I won't get chilled, even though the dry shirt warms my skin. Rob is still shirtless as he refills our bottles.

I suddenly remember the useless flashlight in my pack, remove it, and place it in my drop bag; I can pick it up later. My small light is working fine and I still have a set of extra batteries and a little over eight miles to the highway crossing where I can pick up another light from my crew. After what seems like about three or four minutes of getting ready and sipping on the soup, which I find out later from the time charts is about eight minutes, I decide we must be going again. I rise up and strap on my waist pack, clinching it tightly to eliminate most of the bounce. I feel the added weight of the two full water bottles pulling down on my hips. I walk over to the drink table and slowly down a cup of soft drink and munch on a couple of potato chips, but the food still tastes lousy. I now decide that I will probably survive on water all the way to the finish.

Rob and I walk toward the exit, adjusting our packs and supplies. I see a sign that says that Brown's Bar is five miles away. When we get there it is just over three miles to the highway. As we leave the comfort and warmth of the aid personnel and lighted civilization, I am comforted knowing that one of the most level and smoothest parts of the trail on the entire course will comfort me during the next five miles back into the darkness. I continue on my trek as a night runner.

Somewhere back a couple of days before the race, all the hoopla began leading up to the start of the race, and now many hours later the race is almost over. I've always noticed that special events almost always have that same big buildup, great athletic events like the Super Bowl and the World Series. Often the activities leading up to the event are bigger than the event itself. Then suddenly the main event begins and then just as suddenly it is over.

This race is no different. I arrive with my crew two days before the main event. There are different meetings with the crews and runners, going over the rules, the use of drop points, the conditions of the course, and medical considerations. At some point it becomes almost repetitious and tiring, almost to the point of distracting the runner from the main event itself. All I want to do at this time is get the race started so I can be in my element.

The day before the race the runners go through a pre-race physical, pick up their numbers, check with their crews and pacers to make sure everything is set for the race, and have a final meal the night before the race. Another running friend and I who are doing the race rent a house for ourselves and our crews. Of course, the people who are supporting us are excited and it is difficult to find a moment to just relax and even take a nap. The last afternoon all runners and crews attend a very long meeting where people are introduced, rules are gone over again, and every last detail of the race is finalized.

A critical factor is getting enough sleep before the race, especially two nights before the race. With all the energy flowing around me, this is virtually impossible. The night before the race is one of unsettled and short sleep. I figure I get about four hours of quality sleep before being awakened about 3:15 am to get ready for the 5 o:clock start. Then I will have to run all day and night and get no sleep at all. The entire buildup is daunting to say the least.

Somehow I get through it all and when the countdown begins to the starting gun, it is a great relief that I can finally get away from it all. The most pleasant thought at the moment is that I will have an entire day and maybe more where I won't be bothered again except under my own terms. It seems to be a strange thought to have.

CHAPTER 12
EARLY MORNING ON HIGHWAY 49
(93.4 MILES)

*Success consists of getting up
just one more time than you fall.*
(Saying)

I am a night runner, slinking along under the cover of blackness where no one can observe my pain and fears, where I can hide behind all my frustrations and curse my fate, finally emerging into the light of day in front of the world of humanity acting like all is well with my world.

In my left hand is my guiding light, my flashlight, a small, artificial stick of immense power, my whole body and soul completely dependent on its continued sustained success to radiate a small beam of brilliance which I chase during the infinite, bleak hours. Failure of the torch means failure of my body to find its way to a destination across the miles of desolation. The light feels none of my pain, yet may determine the final outcome of my race.

The night is my ally; I can fight against it and it becomes an invisible, soul-tearing devil trying to drag me down to the depth of despair and disappointment. I can run with it as my partner and win my race. It slows me down, but I need slowing down, my determination mellowed and braked back to conserve strength to complete the challenge. It cools the daytime heat by covering the sun, making my vigor and zeal renewed along with the new, fresh, soft night air. It tries to make me tired, to make me sleepy, but this effect makes me concentrate at a higher pitch to stay awake, to avoid those pitfalls that await to trip me up on the trail.

The trail conjures up strange illusions when mixed with my flashlight. The rocks do not appear very sharp, their usual distinct daytime surfaces appearing as shadows blurred by the mixture of darkness and the weakened glow of the light. My footsteps become more and more precarious as I have trouble noticing the danger of each rock, but for some strange, almost non-physical explanation, I negotiate with almost feathery steps the blurry obstacles in the trail without tripping or slowing down.

The uphill and downhill sections appear more suddenly. I can see only a short distance ahead, as the narrow beam, along with my eyes, intently concentrates just a few feet ahead of each step to ensure each foot plant is made flawlessly. Suddenly the trail juts upwards steeply only a few short strides ahead of my light. I point the shimmering, narrow ray on the hill to see how far I have to go, leaving me temporarily blinded to the trail just in front of my feet. I keep my eyes darting back and forth, alert for any strange, night creatures that might reach out and grab me.

At night I wear my glasses to enhance the clarity of objects, my somewhat blurred vision not affected during the bright sharpness of the daytime sunlight. As I work up a hill, I perspire slightly and the lenses of my glasses fog up around the edges. I use my finger to try to wipe them clear, further smearing up the dust that has already collected on the lenses. Straps on the frame attach around and to my head, securing the glasses firmly to my face. Reflections from the trail and light bounce at odd angles off the dirt smeared on my lenses, creating UFO-like images darting across my field of vision.

I run on in the night, my small light leading the way, a tiny spot in a forest of vegetation, the wicked darkness of the hidden trail hammering at my soul, trying to darken it in its likeness by telling it that there is just too much work ahead, that my body cannot handle the pain to complete the task. The darkness calls for me to quit, begging me to stop, yelling at me that it is hopeless. The darkness will never end; I can't escape it for the rest of the race. If the black sky fades out and the sunlight returns I have lost my race. I must succeed in the darkness, through the night, the endless forever stretching of the miles on the narrow ribbon of trail with the only lights in my soul of hope and with the little hand light helping to comfort me. The darkness implores me that I can't do it, that I will succumb to its rays, the rays of a gut-deep, never ending trail.

Running in the dark from one place on the trail to another seems endless. The trail just rolls on; the clock seems to stop, to take forever. Yet time moves quickly and my next destination is not in sight, and I know I am losing the battle. The darkness is laughing at me, goading me to panic. I gently bite my lip and continue on, refusing to answer his threats.

The shadows in the night deepen into a darker, hellish blackness and grab for me. The flashlight plays strange tricks to my eyes, the shadows of small plants and bushes darting by me as my body and flashlight move forward and bounce up and down all at once, conjuring up images of small mice running by my feet. The plant becomes a rolling log, a falling rock. A bear hunkers ahead of me on the trail, ready to devour me in huge death-like jaws. A shadow snake slithers across the trail, breaking the beat of my rhythmic stride. My pacer and I don't discuss it often, but I know he sees these monsters of the shadows too. He lets it slip once that he thinks he sees an animal moving across in front of him, but that it is only a shadow from his light. We must talk occasionally to scare the monsters away, so we won't trip over the invisible beings with fangs and jaws.

The darting lights of other runners ahead offer some comfort. These small beams flashing back and forth make it appear the runners are engaging in some wild dance. Movement seems up and down, not forward. The shadows of the runners go from large to small and back to large again, depending on the shifting lights, the alterations in speeds, and the changing from uphill to downhill. They seem far away but are very close, their shadows playing tricks with my mind receiving their sight signals. We gain on them quickly, so quickly we almost barrel into them and pass them as they step off to the side of the trail to let us pass by. Their faces are merely skeletons in the darkness, their identities blurred completely as ghosts by the night tides.

I finally allow my soul to accept the night. It then becomes my friend, because I am not able to see how far I have yet to go. I run on, one step at a time, the present straightaway, the next curve, the dip in the trail my only goal. I can't see off in the distance, which is the best medicine for my mind and soul, because I don't need to see how far I have yet to go. In the darkness I plan only the next few steps, the next minute, and this is the only way my movement can be if I expect to finish this race. The darkness becomes my built-in patience string, my rope pulling on my straining body, holding me back from going too fast, from becoming the hare. I must remain the tortoise to the finish. I must get there, and the darkness puts its gentle shield over me and softly holds me back.

I pad along softly on the trail, the air cool wafting, my body relaxed, my eyes intensely concentrating on each step in the dimly lit blackness of the night shade. My legs ache like they never have before, but that ache is anchored in the dark recesses of my mind, and I plunge each step, one awkward stride at a time, in a distorted shuffle, the dark automation of muscles responding to what they have been doing all day and now all during the night. The muscles have forgotten the pain in the darkness, as my mind envelops the warm blackness as my friend, my closest friend. As long as my friend stays with me all the way to the finish, I will win my race.

I talk to the night, trying to convince it to remain, to always and forever be my friend. To become my enemy is to invite death, to invite failure. We are on intimate terms, sharing my pains and agonies. It must stay with me to the end. The stars wink down at me, reminding me that the night and I are still together, reaching and grasping unitedly. I am a night runner. The enemy night is no longer my enemy. The night is my friend; I run with the night forever.

Just after the weigh-in and leaving the Auburn Lakes Trail checkpoint, I suddenly become ill again. I stop just outside the exit of the checkpoint to urinate, the bright flood lights still casting their eerie beams through the dark woods. All of a sudden I vomit without any warning at all. The awful thrust inside my stomach bolts upward, and I am helpless to stop the heaving. I do it twice but I can't get anything to come up; I am bent over double trying to regain precious control. It hits me so suddenly I can hardly believe it happens. There is no warning, no upset stomach, nothing coming up in my throat right before it happens. The only thing that comes up at all is the taste of coke. I drank some coke only a couple of minutes ago.

I notice that Rob abruptly stops and looks back at me. I can't see his face, but I sense by his posture that he is worried. He is suddenly quiet and waits very patiently, and I feel an instant of concern radiating from him. He later tells me that it is one of the biggest points of anxiety he has the entire time he runs with me.

I glance back to see if we are out of range of the aid station. No one there seems to notice what happens as no human shadows come out into the woods to see what the matter is. I am sure I am too far away for them to hear me, plus the noise of the generators, the constant talking, and busy activity helps drown out any noises. At this point I determine to show Rob that I am really all right. Just as after the other time I become sick back at Volcano Canyon, the sickness seems to relieve the pressure in my stomach, and I suddenly breathe easier and the muscles relax throughout my entire body. The brief stop at the aid station has settled my legs.

Rob starts walking as I follow on the flat, gentle trail meandering through the woods on the side of a ravine. Both of us know that I am still on a sub-24 hour pace, but we sense instinctively that I am starting to cut the time too close for comfort. Within my swirling, somewhat confused mind I suddenly make a clear, decisive evaluation. My legs feel reasonably well at this point, my stomach is better than it has been for a long time, the trail is easy going, and the air is cool. I tell Rob to start running and to pick up the pace. I will follow right on his heels, and he is to not stop for anything. Off through the woods we tear like two frightened animals.

As we progress there becomes a certain calculated steadiness about our run. The increased speed stretches out our tightening muscles. We gently brush by vegetation, hop over rocks, slide down and up short banks, flash our lights ahead to check for footing, yellow ribbons and the green florescent sticks oddly glowing in the blackness. I stay 15 to 20 feet behind him so I can see trouble spots on the trail; any closer and I might not see some offending obstacle in time to avoid tripping. Rob's waist pack continues to bounce, as he is still unable to get it tight enough. His stride is slightly bouncing in itself, and this only accentuates the problem. The rhythm of the jouncing pack is like soft, soothing music, a sort of hypnotic quality as we continue to shuffle quickly along, somehow maintaining our footing.

On and on we go, passing several slower runners in the process. We stop and walk a couple of short uphill sections, but in my memory I don't remember very clearly those walking sessions. My legs begin to ache more and more the longer we run, but I don't want to stop until we reach that next checkpoint. I focus my eyes to the surface of the trail to concentrate on each distinct step, and I hone my mind to tell myself that my legs aren't heavy and that there is no pain. I fix my mind power toward my legs, willing them to feel as light as feathers. My thoughts are in a somewhat self-induced hypnotic trance, willing my legs to move forward in a syncopated pace in tune with the undulations of the trail.

We pound doggedly onward, the trail seemingly endless, but we never allow ourselves to let up. We know our goal is just around the next corner, or perhaps the next one, somewhere in the continuous, endless night. I am running now on automatic, and my thoughts toward feathers actually seem to physically put more energy into my legs. The most forgiving help here is that the trail is level the entire distance, and the footing is very smooth and forgiving.

I am in perfect rhythm with the trail for those five miles about 85 to 90 miles into the race. I don't try to explain from where I really receive my energy; I simply accept it as fact. There are no unseen forces holding me back. As my mind drifts with the darkness, suddenly we round a bend and see lights ahead of us. In one respect I expect the aid station sooner than it comes, yet at the same time I have the contradictory surprise feeling that it is here too soon. We have covered over five miles in way under an hour, and our clocks are approaching 2 a.m. We have just about ten miles to go to the finish line and just over three hours to make it under 24 hours.

I am exhausted as we reach the aid station, and I know that we have a difficult hill somewhere ahead during the next short 3.3 miles to the Highway 49 crossing. I spend a few minutes resting, take my pack off, and have Rob refill my bottles. Mine are not completely empty, but he tops them off. My small, backup flashlight is still working on its original batteries, so I know I will have plenty of light to continue. Quickly we end our stay and take off again. After a minute or so of jogging, I discover I have left a small pocket off my waist pack at the aid station, and the extra batteries for the flashlight are inside. Rob tears back to find the batteries while I continue on ahead. I play a game to see how far I can progress before Rob catches back up to me. Within about five minutes I see his light approaching from behind. He has returned with the lost batteries and my pocket.

For the first time in the race, I comprehend, I mean really know, that I can definitely make it under 24 hours. All I need to do is keep moving at a steady, but unhurried pace. I understand that I must contain myself, and I command myself to keep doing what I have been doing, taking one step, one mile at a time. I can't look ahead yet; my race has not reached the finish line. Rob and I discuss the fact that knowing there are fewer than 10 miles remaining in a 100 miler is a tremendous mental boost; the countdown at last is toward zero in the right hand column.

After a short, level stretch Rob and I seem to be surrounded by all kinds of other runners and pacers, lights flashing in undisciplined fashion across the terrain like a mixture of unsynchronized floodlights all glaring at once.

A strange phenomenon in this race is that at one moment we are alone, often for long periods of time, and then suddenly runners seem to appear everywhere on the trail. Soon after leaving the aid station, we barrel down a steep hill which puts us fairly close to the river, at least so we can hear the water cascading down the canyon off somewhere fairly distant in the night darkness. We slide recklessly, kicking up dirt, as we drop down the precipitous old dirt road.

I really feel the physical tiredness now, but I am bolstered both physically and mentally by knowing where I am and how much time I have left to make my deadline. We start walking and slow jogging on a rolling road, most of it uphill. Once again on the uphill several runners pass us. Finally the trail breaks off to the left and starts up a very steep one mile climb or more to the highway, where our crew will be waiting for us. That new reality of the nearness of my friends bolsters my spirit.

I walk slowly up the hill, content to conserve myself, not to do something stupid to cause an injury with such a short distance remaining. I talk

Easy running along a ridge.

to myself, telling me to be patient as a couple of runners pass by me, actually running up the steep incline. Rob walks much faster than I do, and soon gets so far ahead of me that I can barely see him, a shadow slinking ahead of me in the blurry mixture of night, sky light, and flashlight beams. I yell at him that I am coming, but that I'm not going to turn this into a sprint yet.

In reality the hill isn't tremendously long in actual distance, probably about a mile, but it seems to go on forever at this point in the race. Appearing out of the dark a man dressed in an Army uniform passes us walking down the hill, practically ignoring us. I know that the National Guard mans the aid station at the top of the incline, so we must be getting close. I take a big swig of water from one bottle to empty it as much as possible. Finally the trail steepens in a sudden, hellish gesture into an almost vertical gully and becomes almost open to the night sky with no trees and little vegetation.

I recognize this spot as being near the top. I carefully plant one foot in front of the other, pushing down with all my strength, thus propelling myself upward. I even put my hands on my thighs and push down to give them some extra added support. I can hear cars and voices above me, and oddly another runner actually runs by me with his pacer up this vertical cliff. I can barely see Rob up ahead, but he has stopped and is waiting for me.

Suddenly we are on top of the hill, and the whole place is bursting with almost sleepy-like activity. My crew is there again, all of them looking somewhat tired at 2:45 in the morning; either that, or the strange lights just produce a mirage. I step on the scale next to a giant, open tent for the last time before the finish. I am two pounds under at 170, but it is still nothing to worry about. At least there are no more scales before the finish. Surprisingly my backup flashlight is still working; I haven't had to change the little AA batteries yet, but I worry because I have only that one extra set.

I ask my crew member Bob if he has another light, and the one he produces is exactly like the one that blew a bulb many miles back, which is now in the drop bag at the last station. He thinks it is mine. I tell him it isn't but I take it with me anyway. Later on, no one claims the flashlight, but my broken one is still in the drop bag. It is like the miracle of the flashlights. It just seems to materialize out of midair; perhaps it is the brother of my original.

My crew gets me refilled and I swig down some water. I am tired of the taste of food and my replacement drink and refuse everything but water at this point. All of the guardsmen are decked out in their military uniforms and are very giving and helpful to the runners; I see a couple of other runners, their pacers, and other busy crews. I feel almost like a general in the middle of these aid station personnel.

We have plenty of time to make the 24 hour deadline and only 6.6 miles to go, granted with one short hill and a long last pull out of the American River Canyon. But with two hours and 15 minutes things are looking good. I can't believe I have just over a 10K left to reach the finish. My crew knows too that everything is under control, and they say they will see me at the finish line before five o'clock. They don't seem particularly excited about it, but perhaps they are too tired to openly express their joy. Maybe their biggest joy is that the race will soon be over so they can get some sleep.

Thinking about it later, I am sure that they worry that something drastic might happen; I should have positively assured them that I would be there before the 24 hour deadline. Even though in my heart I know I will make it, I don't want to say anything until the stadium is in sight.

I say one last farewell to my crew, and Rob and I grope in the darkness mixed with lanterns and lights from other crews for the correct way back on to the trail. One crew member steers us in the right direction, and we leave them for the final time. During this last section we will visit a couple of small aid stations, but I have been over this section many times in training sessions and know the trail very well, all of its ups and downs, and I feel that for the first time all day I am on my way home at last.

Just as I leave this aid station I must cross Highway 49, an asphalt road of two lanes with a white line down the middle. The fact of the highway registers only briefly with me at the time. Although there was a paved highway at Foresthill, we never actually ran on it. This is the only time the runners actually step on a real highway, and Highway 49 is one of the oldest and most recognizable highways in the state of California, one that winds through the historic gold country, up and down and twisting around for several hundred miles.

The good thing about highways is that they take you along specific paths to specific destinations. They are essential to finding our ways in life paths. Yet that is also the main deficiency of a highway. The road goes to a specific destination and we must stay on it until we get to where we are going. If we leave the highway for some other road, we will not end up where we had intended to go. To get our specific destination, we must stay on that highway at all costs.

That is why it is a relief when I get back on the trail. The trail also appears to have a destination, and certainly in this race that is so very true. Whereas along the highway the sole purpose is the destination, along the trail another purpose enters into the fray: the journey itself. The trail wanders all over the place, sometimes presenting tough obstacles, sometimes flowing gently across the landscape without a care. I feel less secure on the trail but I am happier because I can take in every nuance of the journey itself, like an adventure that has something new with each corner that I turn. The trail is full of surprises, some discouraging, but most likely joyful in some way. The trail has a sense of humor and sends rocks rolling or makes you wade through a stream. But you laugh along with the trail and in the end it treats the runner with respect.

Many have used the highway or road as a metaphor for life. I prefer my metaphor of life to be the trail, for it is never dull and has so much more vitality and energy.

CHAPTER 13
NO LEGS AT NO HANDS BRIDGE
(96.6 MILES)

Far in the pillared dark
Thrush music went -
Almost like a call to come in
To the dark and lament.

But no, I was out for stars;
I would not come in.
I meant not even if asked,
And I hadn't been.
(Robert Frost)

I have two hours and ten minutes to make it just over six and a half miles to the finish, and I know victory is within my grasp, if only I can just hang on; that is all, hang on. Rob and I depart from the Highway 49 aid station, jog down the road to the crossing and pad silently across the pavement to the gate on the other side. I feel like I'm stepping on a clean kitchen floor as I touch the smooth asphalt with my reddish-brown foot covers that pass for shoes. We wend our way at a slow shuffle along a rolling section of soft trail outlined by grasses and darkened woods. Two flashlights appear rearward and quickly overtake us as we step to the side of the trail to let them file by.

I begin the hike up a medium steep grade toward a field of wild, breeze-whipped grasses at the top of a hill, at which point it is downhill for just under three miles to No Hands Bridge. I tell Rob not to hurry as he saunters quickly ahead of me until he is almost out of sight. I know he is trying to get me to speed up, but my burning thighs won't respond to speed now. The pain on the sides of each leg reduces me to a shuffling walk, a technique which allows me to proceed with a minimal dull, throbbing ache. I know it is only a short distance to the top of the hill, but it seems longer in my current agonizing, physical state.

My feet are nailed to the ground; dull, radiating and torturous jabs of heavy pain zap against and into my thick thigh muscles, the solid working quadriceps pulling me for hours along the up and down trail. Thousands of times I lift one leg, then the other, effort turning to such torture that I must turn my mind to other thoughts merely to stifle this brutality that I must suffer mile after mile, beyond any normal sensible, human endurance.

I must make believe that there is no pain. Damaged muscles cry for relief, the permanent relief of completely stopping, of stretching out and saying no. The pain becomes an invisible blur of nothingness; I blot it out so I may continue. I must will the lifting of each leg just enough to clear the dirt and rocks, to shove the leg and following body forward by a couple of more feet; I repeat the rote movement countless times, until my reflexes take over.

Cursing softly at the screaming throb relieves my mind only for a fleeting moment, temporarily hiding painful, stark reality. I must concentrate my vision on the next spot, lifting and planting, lifting and planting, in rhythm to an endless, physical tune that keeps going in a perfect, agonizing tempo. I must accept this throbbing as my ally to make my fate. It tells me where I stand at this point. If I can bear it at all, I keep moving. Quitting is no reality, only if I am seriously injured. My companion is pain, and I can travel together with him in a joyless, but comfortable bliss.

Surprisingly the time passes rapidly, and soon the trail levels out and becomes a two track road across a green, grassy field where we must follow the yellow ribbons and green flares carefully as the tracks are almost completely covered by the lush grasses. We can choose either of the dual tire paths narrowly carved into the thousands of flowing, green strands. We pick the left one for no particular reason and break into a stiffening jog across the field. Up ahead the bright spotlight of the very small Painted Rocks aid station looms mysteriously in the black, like some small way station amidst an underworld hell.

We arrive at the station where there are only a few people sitting at a table with some cups of soft drinks and a few food items. They seem almost suspended in trances, distorted shadowy forms reposing almost stiffly in their nightly domain. My ears hear their voices, but my mind sees only silent mummies strapped to chair-like tombs. Rob grabs a soft drink and swigs it down while I stand silently and take nothing, my cravings for food and drink almost completely gone. I can make it in now with the liquid in my two bottles. We thank them and trod onward.

The trail begins its downhill slide now, with a couple of brief, short uphills and some level spots. We catch and pass two pairs of flashlights very quickly and weave through the trees and brush along the green-lighted path. I again notice these little flares seem further away than they really are. We see them in the distance in the woods and run toward them when suddenly we are on top of them. I realize that they are so much smaller than what our minds say they are; we think we see them off in the darkness, when in reality we can reach out and almost touch them. From seemingly far distances they are suddenly on top of us like exotic little spaceships, flickering their eerie, tiny, green flashes of welcome. I wonder if the little green men inside know just how crazy we are out here.

I move along the trail at a running gait whenever the trail dips downhill or levels off, but I know I must look like an old lady shuffling around a track trying hard to finish my one lap. Each step brings searing pain shooting up through my upper body and striking my brain like a clash of symbols. I think only of arriving at No Hands Bridge and the fact that each step brings me closer to the finish where the silver buckle awaits me. I can't do anything foolish now, but I must not stop to walk too often, for fear that I may not be able to start running again. Each moment I must start again is like jump starting my legs, trying to produce a spark to restart my muscles again. Each time the agony of that initial jogging step jars my soul with racking doubt. My confidence of making it is painfully strong, but I know I'm not there yet and have some work ahead of me. Silver images flash before my eyes in the darkness.

Pain now becomes my ally. I know it is biting me to the core, but I concentrate on it as a good feeling, one that is urging me on. Each beat of my heart brings on a beat of pin-sharp pain. I drag my legs along with my upper body; somehow I am still moving; somehow I don't sprawl over the trail into a mass of nothingness, melding with the trail and fading to air like Dorothy's witch.

I can locate no specific spot of throbbing agony anymore. From my waist on down is one solid cramping spasm. Somewhere my instinct, my will, my piercing, burning anguish transfers itself outside my body and rides along with my concentrating mind. In my inner recesses of faint but clear consciousness I recall walking on a narrow, rocky ledge high above a rushing maelstrom of foaming water below me. Every step must be perfect; balance must be there totally or I will tumble to my death. I cannot look down for fear of dizziness, toppling, falling, falling, losing consciousness, sleep. Each step now is only recorded by the gnawing pain, each stride feeling one spasm on the edge of that ledge in the corner of my brain. The wrong pain will topple me and forever tumble my body into the death of my race.

Powering my way through this nightmare with my pitiful strides keeps me awake and alert. It is after three in the morning, but I am wide awake. Sleep is something I can engage in later when the race is over; I don't have time for her now. I have never been so mentally alert as at this point in the conquest. In fact, despite the hours of running during normal sleeping hours, this is the first real time it has consciously occurred to me that I should be succumbing to sleep at this ungodly hour. Sleep just hasn't been a negative factor for me.

We now run above the twisting, two lane highway, and Rob comments that there are sure a lot of vehicles for this time of the morning. I respond that they are probably those of crew members coming and going from the highway crossing. The engine of a nighttime truck splatters the night air with a raucous crack as it rounds a curve and accelerates down the hill 100 feet or more below us under our feet off the bank to our right. Headlights flash across the dark in no particular formation, like some spotlight seeking out a needle in a haystack of darkness in front of it. I imagine hiding from a dangerous enemy with deadly guns seeking to destroy us. The darkness of the woods protects us from any harm.

I check my watch and our time is still holding; I've run this section of the trail many times and know it well. We cross the newly fixed section from a recent flood, crossing a wide, flat, slightly downhill section in a clearing directly above the highway. It is a straight, unobstructed drop down to the pavement, and we cautiously walk this section, even though it is very wide and safe.

We are on the trail and running again, rounding the bend toward the drop-off down to No Hands Bridge. We trudge carefully around the side of the hill which falls quickly away to our right. The path narrows as it hugs the bank, vegetation becoming sparser. I can hear the sound of the river as it gets closer, the same old familiar rushing sound, only deeper throated, like some dear companion telling me that I am almost home. I know I'm almost there now, and I can't believe I may actually win the buckle.

We haven't seen another runner for ten minutes or more now, but I know there are others close by also desperately trying to make the finish, many feeling warm and comfortable now like me. I am still wearing my jacket, still unzipped, and my shirt is wet again with perspiration. My glasses still periodically fog up, with the wiping of the lenses with my fingers becoming an unconscious, automatic, and somewhat futile gesture.

By concentrating on the other things around me besides my running, I become conscious that the aching is now less severe, although still ever present as a reminder of my task. Light and trail mix together; trail no longer exists. I seem to flow in suspended, slow motion in rhythm to a slow song, but I play harmony with each less cramping stride, no longer crying pitiful inner cries, but only bearing my cross majestically as a soldier called to defend his homeland. I lift my chest slightly and breathe in deeply the cooling, summer air. The squeaking of our packs and the scraping of our shoe bottoms against the trail are the drums in the rhythm section of my tune.

I abruptly hear subdued, inarticulate voices and see floodlights directly below us. Our lights pick out the rough trail and the steep curves to the bridge. Large rocks and uneven ruts from the soft, brown dirt litter the quickly descending path. A voice below us calmly notes that another couple of runners are coming, and I realize they mean us. Rob leads the way to the checkpoint, and at first I believe they think he is the runner and I am the pacer. When Rob is leading me, I can understand their reasoning, but by now I don't really care.

We pause for a moment on the bridge to exchange comments before starting on our last leg. A man with a small flashlight informs us that it is about 40 minutes to the finish line; looking at my watch we have one hour and 20 minutes to make it. I want to shout with joy, but I am afraid my legs might answer back by telling me to advance no more. I now understand the expression when someone says he is on his last legs. I have gone way past my last legs; my mind tells me I must continue, that there must be something left in those limbs to get me up that last hill to Auburn.

I am about to embark to the top of my Everest, my culminating peak of conquest, to the highest point on the earth. From here on I become a one step at a time being, each movement forward bringing me a few feet closer to my rainbow. Time is not important anymore; I have plenty stored in reserve. The entire patience of the race is now reduced to one single, small hill coming out of one small canyon, a mere gentle tug up the side of the wall.

No Hands Bridge during daylight hours. Sub-24 hour finishers cross it in darkness.

Everything is behind me. I understand the real awesomeness of the journey I have just completed as I prepare to bring it in to its culmination. My friend, that magnificent trail with its beautiful song, is about to finish its seemingly endless album. I will miss my friend. Have I conquered him and have I really formed a forever lasting truce with him? Somehow I know deep inside that we will meet again and do it together one more time.

I know I can make it now by walking almost all of it if I have to. I know I can walk, no matter how badly it hurts. I realize now that the only thing that can stop me is if I have to crawl. I also know that crawling can still be a remote possibility, that I can't start celebrating just yet. I must muster every last ounce of strength I have. Now I completely understand what really being mentally tough is all about. My mental incentive to make it gives me renewed energy. Somewhere way down deep inside my body, all those months of training and those extra miles of moving when I wanted to call it a day, will produce for me an extra reserve of power that will put me past my final goal. I will not give in now, no matter what I may meet on my final journey to the stadium.

Rob and I cinch up our belts and begin the first steps of the last leg of our long victory home. The lights of the city and the relief from the agony reach out with their arms and beckon me forward. I begin the few thousand remaining, joyful, agonizing steps to the finish line.

There are those few moments in life when after all the preparation to conquer some obstacle to reach a very high goal, we realize that we are actually going to do it, even though we still have a little work to do before the completion. The euphoria by this time can carry us to the completion because the final result is inevitable. These moments in life are very rare, but they keep us butting our heads against the seemingly impossible completion of a task.

The one thing about the completion of such a task is that we are often in disbelief that it is final over and we have succeeded because all along we didn't know for sure what the outcome would be. Suddenly we have reached the pinnacle of success in some endeavor and we really don't believe it for a moment. At this point in the race I knew I was going to be successful, that I only had to walk the rest of the way and I would make it. There was no doubt at this moment that I would make it under 24 hours.

These are the moments in life that we hold suspended in our memories forever. I distinctly remember 20 years after the event that at the time I was thinking that I really wanted to enjoy the entire moment because it would probably never happen again in my life. I wanted the entire last hour of the race and beyond to not come to an end; I wished that time could be suspended and I could enjoy it forever. In a mere 24 hours after the completion of the race, life would go on to its next trail.

The clarity of the ending has remained with me over all those years, just as other great endings in life have also done so. As I get older I find it harder to find those moments and they may pale in comparison to the one I felt in this race, but they have been there in all their glory.

I remember coaching in a final high school football playoff championship game and realizing we had it won with just a minute to go as we fell on the ball. I remember my first trip to Whistler ski area and riding the lift just before standing on the top of the mountain for the first time, with a gigantic vista spread out before me. I remember completing my first book and anticipating seeing it in print for the first time. The moments are rare. The knowledge that I was to be successful in this race stands out as maybe number one in all my life's experiences.

CHAPTER 14
THE FINAL PUSH
(99.5 MILES)

*The man taught enough by life's dream of the
    rest to make sure;
By the pain-throb, triumphantly winning
    intensified bliss,
And the next world's reward and repose, by the
    struggle in this.*

                                        (Robert Browning)

As Rob and I slowly trot across the smooth, dirt surface of No Hands Bridge, I now know that victory is mine, just 3.4 miles and an hour and 20 minutes or less away. This single lane, old retired structure spans high above the deep, gentle American River below it. Once without hand railings, thus its name, recent years have brought forth fences along the sides that prevent runners from possibly stumbling off the sides to certain death far below. Several months previous to the race floods wash over the top of the bridge, but somehow it survives to maintain its creaky domain over the river. During the warm afternoon summer hours, countless sunbathers and swimmers spread across the boulders on the river's banks, reposed in relaxing do-nothing activities. Between three and four in the morning the revelers sleep in their beds, unaware of the passing drama dominating their private realms.

My thighs are beyond aching at this point. I feel pricks of deep burning sensations like small fires flaring inside my muscle tissue, and the tightness is like steel rods running right down the middle of my upper legs. Using my muscles to lift the legs to bend the knees in order to run pulls on every fiber in my thighs, like the stretching of iron bands rather than the once limber rubber bands of the previous morning. I shuffle rather than run, barely able to elevate my feet, but somehow I avoid tripping on the dirt and rocks. I clear the dangerous trail with my shoes by mere fractions of an inch.

We move momentarily along the trail in this fashion before I insist to Rob that I absolutely must take a walking break, even though the trail is level. I turn quickly and glance back across toward the bridge and canyon behind me and see no lights following us. Rob tries vainly to encourage me to run on the level section, but I have practically given up by now. I shuffle for a minute or two and then break down to walk for several more minutes. I have no purposeful incentive now to push myself because I know I will make it no matter what speed I employ.

Perhaps I want to savor my personal victory for just a little while longer. I have worked so long for this race; I have spent almost 24 hours out here on this adventure, suffering in so many new and unique ways, yet attaining never reached before periods of joy. Those lights of bliss now flash gleefully before my eyes. Perhaps I am afraid that the race might end too soon. I know I will welcome the finish line, but I also know I may never experience such joyous pain and accomplishment again in my life, at least not in the same way as I now do. For a moment time stands still, but it must move forward. I wish I can capture it forever on my mind film, to rerun over and over again in future time warps whenever I so desire. I have told myself that the race itself is the goal, not the finish, that I don't really want to my race to end.

Maybe I am afraid that something unpredictable and unnecessary may happen to keep me from the finish line if I really attempt to push the pace now. My body is at a point of delicate balance; I must still keep my patience, my race of one step at a time. I am definitely now thinking of the finish line, and I want to play the game far behind the red line of danger so I will actually arrive there safely. Probably the real reason I won't push it is that I'm just plain exhausted; I have planned and trained for 100 miles, not for even one more mile than that, and I have now almost completed the distance; my body is trying to tell me that I am running out of fuel. The true impenetrable wall looms darkly around each turn in the trail, to be pushed back just a little bit one more time again and again.

The last section of the trail before hitting the streets of Auburn curves out of the canyon in a series of ups and downs through little mini-canyons, sometimes for only a couple hundred feet. There are several short rough sections over rocks and uneven dirt where the spring landslides from the floods have caused a mess of rubble. Rob and I pick our way carefully through these sections.

After each rough section comes a short, smooth, flat section of former rail roadbed where I do my only running. We know one of the uphill sections signifies the last climb to the pavement, but I have forgotten which one here in the dead of the blackness. We start up one section, Rob saying he believes it is the last uphill. I know instinctively from my training runs that we are here too soon even as I become hopeful. I block out disappointment when I realize I am right in my evaluation and advance patiently on to the next level section.

Finally we reach the steep switchback section, and even though it is a relatively short distance, I walk it. I see two lights flashing chaotically through the trees just below us and hear unintelligible, light-hearted voices. Another runner and his pacer soon come roaring by us but I have absolutely no desire to try to race this competitor to the finish because the race is still within myself, and I know I am going to win that race, the only one that actually counts.

Rob is moving more quickly than I am and opens up a fairly large gap between us. I yell at him that I can't go any faster but that I'm still making it at my pace. I see his light playing with the shadows up ahead of me on the trail. The runner who has recently passed me crosses way up above me high on the switchbacks, and I see and at the same time hear another runner and his pacer approaching from below me, their staccato chatter brushing the pre-dawn stillness.

Finally Rob stops and waits for me; his light pauses and freezes on the trees just above me. We reach a little clearing of burnt brush and trees, the sick, ragged remnants from a small fire, and I know we are nearing the top of the canyon. We step on to an almost level road and move forward at a jog-shuffle for a few short moments. Then the road splits, to the left the trail section used in last year's run, to the right the last few hundred yards to Robie Point, the asphalt paved section of residential road leading one and a half miles to the finish line. A runner and his pacer behind us catch up with a fast walk and pass me, and we saunter up the last steep section together with great new anticipation of the road.

Ahead in the rays of our darting lights, I observe a green metal gate crossing the road. We go around the right side, four of us in a line. I am last in the group, and a bird suddenly bursts up out of the middle of the hollow green post with a splatter and throb of vigorous, tiny wings. The others hear the sound, and I explain to them what it is. A nest inside the post is obviously the home of the bird. I wonder what these birds might be thinking, being constantly disturbed all night long. We can hardly know the nightmare they must endure every few minutes, their peace being constantly shattered in a world where peace is the only byword. Then again, perhaps we do comprehend the wild, night dream, for we all experience it in the endless hours of searching for our destination.

The gate just before Robie Point, with less than two miles to go.

We go around the corner and I hear voices. We now see the street lights at Robie Point and observe a large group of people manning this last ditch aid station. They offer us aid, but all the aid I desire is at the finish line, so with rings of encouragement in our ears, Rob and I take off in an even paced stroll up the paved road.

For a half mile, the road is very steep; it is a narrow lane and a half road that winds along a ridge, punctuated by occasional eerie, dim-bulbed street lights yawning tiredly and an occasional lone spectator. Homes nestle back unobtrusively into deep, dark woods and vegetation, not tract homes, but each home attractively having its own unique size, form, and individual signature. Some are small and quaint, while others are large and stately. The setting is one of dreamlike bliss, and in the darkness of early morning shadows cast from the street lamps, we exist in an almost unreal sense of presence that no one really lives here.

We come to a crossroad right before the last climb where several people stand on the side of the road applauding. I glance around me and realize several runners and their pacers are striding up the hill along with us, some slightly ahead, others slightly behind. On the trail I can't identify runners when they pass me in the dark, but out here under these artificial lights I recognize a young red-haired woman that I had seen at least once previous during the race sometime during the daylight hours which now seem to have passed from existence many days ago.

I walk comfortably the last few steps of the uphill section. The road levels out as it turns to the right. I hesitantly inform Rob that I am ready to try to run again. As I lift my legs to move, stiffness envelops my entire lower extremities like some violent, arthritis attack. I suddenly feel like a car needing a complete overhaul, but trudge ahead at a snail's pace, placing one foot closely in front of the other. Walking deliberately and unconcerned on the road ahead is another runner and his pacer, talking in feeling animation. They ignore us as we pass them, totally engrossed in their own pending celebration of victory as they march toward the coveted finish line.

The road curves to the left, dips a little, straightens out; yellow trail ribbons almost litter the limbs of trees and bushes, clearly marking the last mile on the road. Ahead I see the last uphill on the course, a small, steep blip that will take only a few seconds to negotiate. I realize with some sadness and at the same time unrestrained joy that this is my very last climb, my final upward push with my crying muscles. My cousins live near the spot, but I don't see them down the road where they live. I struggle with my running and finally decide on one last short walk along the last level section and up the last short rise.

Suddenly on our left a woman standing behind a fence in the front yard of her modest home begins applauding and cheering us on, informing us that we are almost done. Rob asks her if she has been up for awhile and gets an affirmative response. I feel real genuine warmth for this new fan of mine that I don't even know who has joyfully joined up in the celebration in the early morning darkness to encourage us to the stadium. She has no reason to be up this early, so it certainly is an unnecessary disruption of her normal sleeping. I know her encouragement and care are genuine, that she truly is happy to see all the runners succeed in their quests. She may feel it is really no sacrifice to cheat her body out of a few hours of sleep. She probably looks forward to being a tiny, insignificant part of the race, a lone beacon of positive reinforcement out on a lonely, empty, streetlight lit, quiet residential road on a cool, early summer morning.

I am also suddenly vividly aware that the air is not all so silent. Off to my left several hundred yards partially hidden by tall trees and the fact that they are down at the bottom of a hill, the lights of the stadium penetrate their eerie glow through the black air. I can hear a crackling voice biting the night off in the distance occasionally, but I can't distinguish the jumbled words. It is a deep, gentle, trained voice on the public address system, stretching out into a mellow tone as if trying not to awaken all the sleeping inhabitants in the surrounding neighborhoods.

We walk up the last incline and the railroad overcrossing is now only a few feet ahead of us. I begin jabbering and bubbling to Rob how that I can't believe it is practically finished. I pick up my feet for one last run and as we approach the bridge, I hear a voice, first once, then again. Breaking into my daze I realize my cousin and her husband are standing beside the road. I yell something unintelligent back at them as we approach the bridge.

I have at last come home to stay. With a light heart and even lighter legs, I am about to enter the last downhill jaunt on the road, into the stadium, and around the track to the finishing banner. It is about 4:30 in the morning, over 23 and a half lifetime hours since I started my odyssey, almost 100 miles back across the Sierra Nevada mountains.

As I step off the bridge and head homeward, many different emotions engulf me. The patience I have held tight to for a seeming eternity is no longer necessary. I no longer need to stay calm and keep my pace and race tempo under tight control. The liquids I have been religiously consuming for hour after hour are no longer needed for my survival. I no longer must just put one foot in front of the other, one careful step at a time. I know for sure now that victory is waiting for me with a smile, a chuckle, and open, friendly arms.

Suddenly all the pain in my legs and body vanishes and I am free. I am a bird and spread my wings: I no longer run anymore. I begin my takeoff down the road and fly on the wings of the light, morning air to my destiny with the finish line.

Sometimes I feel like there is a deity even though I can't physically see or touch him. The moment doesn't happen very often. This is one of those special moments in my long life. Perhaps I have felt it other times and couldn't really define it. Sometimes I know that what I am doing is not totally under my control, that there is some other higher force pushing me along. I believe that I find these moments more in physical endeavors than in mental pursuits, although it is possible to find it in the latter.

How do you explain that after 99.5 miles of running and often struggling to make it to the finish, during the last half mile of the race my body felt light and free, almost as if it were detached from the gravity of the earth. There was no pain and I felt no struggle at all to run at this point. There are of course physical and psychological reasons why this happens all the time to athletes, but at some moment the athlete experiences being in another zone, at complete peace and in total clarity. We see it all the time in big time athletics.

Yet the ordinary person can experience these moments too; I know I did during the last half mile or so of the race. I almost felt as if something other worldly was carrying me to the finish line. The quarterback sees the entire field with clarity in the final drive; the basketball player takes the final shot, knowing it will go in; the pitch looks gigantic and clear as the baseball player hits the game winning home run. The golf hole looks gigantic to the pro golfer as he drains the big put to win the big tournament.

During those last few moments of the race, the trail seemed to consist of air and gentle clouds as it pulled me gently down its surface to its ending. Throughout my life I have continued to look for such moments. That's one of the great motivations to continue to pursue life to its fullest.

CHAPTER 15
THE FINISH
(100 MILES)

When life gives you a wave,
ride it to the end.

(Saying)

The morning streetlights yawn their glaring bulbs across the dipping, winding road, casting hazy shadows of telephone poles, small front yards, picket fences, and cold, night-rested automobiles. Gravity pulls my newly revived, heavy legs down the chipped and uneven asphalt, the dark, plop-slapping, reddish-brown shoes clashing awkwardly with the light black of the cracked, road surface.

No one observes my shoes barely lifting minute inches above the surface with each shuffling step, racks of victorious pain jabbing each leaden thigh on every unsteady, wobbly foot plant. The road twists and plunders down through the eerie semi-darkness like some deranged roller coaster. I intuitively sense, rather than visually observe, people along the sidewalks and in their yards, mere statue-like, sleeping shadows viewing unemotionally the victorious runner, probably wondering what I've been through during my night dream, knowing it to be some dark, intimate secret they will never experience.

Suddenly the gate to the stadium looms ahead of me, the distorted rays of the stadium lights flashing crazily through the openings in the trees and bushes guarding the entrance way. To my left suddenly appears a big man whom I recognize as John, a member of our running club who has traveled over four hours to see the finish. I blubber out some greeting and unbuckle my waist pack hastily, throwing the pack and bottle into his arms. I eagerly yearn to enter the stadium unburdened from my physical restraints as well as my mental shackles.

Rob is still with me, but I have lost the feeling of his physical presence; he is running next to me, but I am no longer aware of his movement. He and John must be exchanging greetings also, but I hear nothing but the quiet crackling of the stadium lights, the bee-like humming of intense bulbs reaching to grasp me, the hush of the stadium crowd, now dwindled to a precious few, hearty inhabitants in the early morning hours when plain mortals are in an unconscious, blissful, heaven-like sleep. Only one quarter of a mile remains to the tape, just one last part of 400 parts that make up my journey. I have come home at last, and my mind is no longer able to focus clearly on the event. Up to now I have been calm and calculating, remembering every nuance of the trail and evaluating every little idiosyncrasy of my body and brain.

My body is numb, my brain suspended. I make a left turn under an archway overhang and then a quick right turn to enter the stadium. My legs are skating on air, and for a brief fraction of a second before I hit the track, I try to analyze why I'm feeling absolutely no body pain or anguish, but my thoughts turn to paralysis as my brain can't comprehend or focus on even the simplest thought. It has kicked into a higher level, floating now high above my body, suspended almost heaven-like, observing the last few seconds of my body's race.

For the first time in my life of competition, I reach a mind-littered crossroads where on the one hand I yearn for my race to end, to be allowed to quit the hours of agonies and never ending painful forward movements, yet on the other hand, hoping there is some way I can suspend time forever, freeze the frame of the finishing lap, perhaps playing the last two minutes in super slow motion, one frame at a time, one second equaling one minute, watching the scene from eyes inside my head, focusing clearly with my brain, absorbing the developing triumph slowly with my heart, my quest for athletic excellence.

The final stadium lap becomes the highlight of my somewhat scattered career as an athlete. My shoes lightly touch down on the packed, dirt track, blurring foot strikes pounding down the silver-laid path toward the finishing banner. The voice of the public address announcer softly blares the finish of another runner ahead of me, and somewhere he mentions something about me, but it is a blurry monologue to my deaf ears; I hear only my heart pounding as I listen to the crackle of heel-nipping, cool air brushing across my face. I glance to my left and running excitedly toward me from the infield is my crew member Paul. I hurriedly rip off my light gray windbreaker and awkwardly fling it toward him as we exchange quickly forgotten comments.

I am now totally unburdened, clad in the basics of running garb, T-shirt, shorts, and shoes, the brisk tingling coolness of the early morning, summer air tugging across my bare arms, my sweat stained, thin, white shirt plastered tightly against my chest. I dip my body slightly to the left, deliberately, but securely round the last turn. My mind is cool and calm as my body clutches the chilly breeze, freeing me from my burden of the no longer endless trail and icing away the many ghosts of the miles and miles of my journey. The track is in clear focus; I see silent, hazy, and outlined waving figures along the side of the track, yelling silent and slow motion cheers of victory.

I meet the halfway mark in the bend of the track, and my eyes perceive in the corner of my pearly vision the blaring glare of the suspended, finishing banner hanging with a tiny flutter on the dirt boundary of the completion gate. The curve begins to straighten, stretching and stretching into tightness, finally jerking into a straight line less than 100 impossibly golden, dirt yards to the ending with welcoming arms of moving, waiting, joyous figures of human shadows.

Somehow on that home stretch I let out a yelp of unrestrained, ecstatic joy, releasing my inner pressure valve, but I can't hear me; I hear only a bare squeak, or perhaps I have gone deaf. The volume of my yelp is like a sigh from the mountain breeze that has been my endless companion. The real yelp is inside my beating heart, my battered but joyful body, within my once concentrating, formerly imprisoned, mind set. I am free from the sentence to the trail, to the thousands of slow, forward steps, the false hopes and agonizing depressions; I am free from the imprisonment of the race. I have challenged and I have prevailed.

The picture in my mind of the last few steps to the finish are impressed forever on my mind, frozen like some time-lapse collage in a future time warp. On the front of my white shirt specifically chosen for the finish line is an artist's drawing of the famous fallen warrior sitting on a horse, and the words from a local race put on by our running club, "The End of the Trail." Never truer were such prophetic words ever written. My trail is now forever ended, but I am not the fallen warrior but a triumphant gladiator. The fallen warrior represents all that my body has lost to achieve this triumph. Yet someday I will become the fallen warrior as I reach the end of life's trail.

I see hazy, steamy lights, a big banner of blurry words, figures yelling and applauding along the side of the track and from beneath the dark, welcoming pit on the other side of the banner; 100 miles of golden trail now fade into this blackness, a welcome relief and a time for rest, but also a bringing of the soul back to the banner of reality, after this long journey through heaven. With one last shuffling lunge, one last raising of my arms and thrusting my fists into the air, my race is over. I cross over into the other world ground of the non-course, the place of mere mortals to celebrate the relief and the joy of eternal achievement.

My first and lasting impression immediately after crossing the finishing line consists of the race co-director, Norman Klein, grabbing me in his arms and relating his joy that I made it. I blubber something about it being my day, but what I really want to say is that I believed I would do it and somehow knew all along that my success would come to pass. All the agony of the pursuit is quickly forgotten while I take a cocky ride on the wings of self-flattery of the accomplishment. It is I, not someone else, who is standing here in success, and I choose to enjoy it without restraint. I see an ABC camera aimed at me as I turn around. My crew and friends are talking fast and furiously, but I can't hear words, only the sounds of celebration.

Someone leads me to a scale and I hear a voice say 168 pounds, down further than it has been all day, but those four pounds don't really matter now. Quickly a woman grabs me, takes my pulse and blood pressure. I am talking machine gun-like almost in senseless bursts and exploding with unrestrained, bounding happiness. My blood pressure is up slightly and the woman asks me to lie down on a cot, which I readily do. One of my crew throws a blanket over me and for the first time in just one day I allow my entire physical body to totally relax.

With the sigh of relief from a totally exhausted body comes a new found peace with the physical environment. In the crispy, morning air I should feel chilled, but my body feels totally comfortable and in tune with the air. I feel no chill at all beneath the light blanket. My friends and crew members keep coming over to talk to me. Nearby I hear the announcer give names and times of runners trying to beat the 24 hour deadline. I make it with less than 26 minutes to spare, but 23 more runners finish in the remaining 26 quick minutes until the piper enters to cut off the flow. I cannot believe that many runners are that close behind me. They suddenly have materialized from nowhere, coming from the same nothingness in a last desperate rush to help share in the triumph at the finish line.

Rob and the author finish again in 1989 in 26:48. This time the sun was high in the sky.

I listen to the race unfold between congratulatory messages from my friends, to the woman who enters the track exactly at 24 hours, but can't reach the finish in time for her buckle. Finally a lady from the scale comes back and rechecks my blood pressure; it has returned completely to a normal reading and I am officially released from the medical tent to leave the finishing area. I don't leave right away. I receive a full massage, comforting and soothing, and I eat some food that easily goes down my calm, settled stomach. I am totally at peace, stiff and sore, but together, totally awake and alert.

Suddenly I notice a new day is dawning. The sky begins to lighten perceptibly and blueness appears in the heavens as the distant sun makes its slow stretch toward the horizon. I agonizingly climb off the cot, using my hands for support, stand stiffly on my wobbly legs, and begin a slow stroll over to a car to take me to a hot shower. I look about me at human figures moving in slow motion around the finishing area in a clear outline in the morning light, an occasional runner now entering the stadium to beat the final 30 hour deadline as a brand new day begins as so many millions have gone before in the rhythmic cycle of time.

The friendly night that protected me for many hours has done its job and is now fading away to this glorious new day, a time of fresh visions, exploratory quests, a new birth of adventure on a new day never before experienced by life. My day, my night are past, gone to oblivion, but forever preserved in my mind and heart of hope, a gentle reminder of my courageous and successful assault to allow my dreams to come true. Seven months of preparation, 24 hours of conquest: the battle and the war is over and I gain victory, not a mere personal conquest, but a total triumph of my entire soul being over the challenge of the trail, my body, my mind. I am home at last and I have secured my conquest.

My official time: 23 hours, 34 minutes, and 47 seconds. I finish in 72nd place; 95 runners finish under 24 hours. My friend Roger finishes in 41st place in 22:30:57. A total of 210 complete the race under the 30 hour deadline. 415 runners began the race; 205 fail to complete the course.

A year later ABC Wide World of Sports produced a show of the 1986 Western States Run. As with all one hour shows, much was left out. It is impossible to capture the true nature of the event, but the producers did a credible job within the limitations they faced. As I sat down that afternoon to watch the account of a race I had completed several months prior, I was wondering what I would see.

In the introduction before the skier comes flying sideways over the jump in the "Agony of Defeat", the beginning of the race was shown with the racers charging toward the mountains. There in a brief second I saw myself with my arms raised, at which point I was faded out. Next several runners were shown crossing the finish line in triumph. Suddenly on the screen arms raised in joy and crossing under the finishing banner was me, number 143, for about a second and a half. At first I couldn't believe that I was actually picked out to appear out of all the others who also crossed the line successfully. Only after the show was over and I could replay the video did I see that I was on a national television show, if only very briefly. I had actually proof on tape of my "Thrill of Victory."

I still have that video of the race, but it has been years since I have replayed it. It just doesn't seem part of me anymore. It is part of my past and I don't need to show off or remember what happened at that moment. In my mind I remember the finish from my mind's eye like it happened yesterday. Twenty years have passed and it seems like it happened yesterday. Every step around the track, the soft voice of the PA announcer in the quiet, early summer morning, the bright lights and crowd of people near the finishing banner, the last easy strides down the finishing stretch, the crossing under the banner and the welcoming words from everyone around me, the elated feeling in my heart, the check out and lying on the cot with my friends offering congratulations: all of it is imprinted forever as a permanent memory on my mind.

For one single day in my days of thousands, I celebrated a great victory, one that would forever change the way I would view life. My journey was over when I crossed under the banner. Yet 20 years later I realize that my real journey had only begun in a much broader and grander scale. The memory of that finish today is printed like a fine motion picture, a memory that will never vanish from my mind, and more important from my life's spirit.

CHAPTER 16
AWARDS AND GLORY

The race is finished, and I have managed to reach the end of the trail in under 24 hours, obviously overjoyed at the success that has come so kindly to me. Although the actual running, the hours of pounding on the trails, is finished, the race will never be completed in my mind. It will remain a significant excerpt of my life forever, permanently branded into my physical and mental consciousness during the rest of my lifetime.

After getting a good breakfast, a long, hot shower, and talking with my crew and cousins for a couple of hours, I finally try to get some much needed rest. As I approach my cousin's home near the course, I see runners still slowly sliding along the road in the penetrating, warm sunlight with their pacers, less than a mile to go before reaching the finish line and completing the race under the 30 hour deadline. My legs are still extremely sore, but the pain is a satisfying one, a badge of my courage to complete the race. These muscles have worked for months now and paid their dues and performed as champions during the race; they will get their due rest and recuperation.

Sleep comes fairly rapidly as I stretch my worn out body on the big double bed with the warmth of the sunlight peaking through the drapes. I slowly but quickly drift off into an intense, deep slumber, my muscles relaxing completely for the first time in over a day. I sleep solidly for about five hours, and when I awaken I feel quite refreshed for some reason, although I know I need more sleep than that.

For a few moments I listen to the silence of the hot, summer afternoon outside the house, the quiet humming of the heat, knowing now that the last of the runners have either completed the course or have dropped out. In a few hours I will attend the awards banquet, to be held outside in a beautiful park-like setting in the early evening after the morning of the finish. I anticipate the awards banquet eagerly because I will be getting the silver belt buckle, the award for finishing the race under 24 hours.

In the shade of the grassy park and on benches, most of the runners, their friends and crew, eat and talk and drink and talk some more for an hour or so before the awards are given out. The mood is relaxed and subdued, but one of anticipation, much like that an hour before the race. People try to locate their drop bags which have been returned from the woods; the bags are dirty, disorganized, looking like they came from some refugee camp. Other people look at pictures and results from the race. At least seven or eight people I got to know during the training for the run didn't finish the race, and a couple of them come by to tell me what happened.

My friend Roger has finished in a fine time of 22 hours and 30 minutes. The others I don't see again and won't see them until some future race where we will meet again. Then we can discuss our fortunes. I gradually notice that my feet are a little sore and there are a couple of cuts on my ankles, but I discover that I have no blisters at all. Other runners are discussing their aches and pains with each other.

The awards ceremony is something that we all wish could go on forever, for it is to honor the successes that we all have attained. After spending months in preparation and 24 hours on the course, the brief moment of getting the award passes too quickly to be appreciated. The ceremony never has the impact of the actual finish of the race, but it is a time to stand, if only briefly, on the pedestal of victory, to receive the accolades of personal achievement. In a way it is an anticlimax to the finish of the event itself, yet it is so important as a validation of the accomplishment.

My entire crew has had to leave to return to their normal work days on Monday, the next day. Roger, of course, is there along with his family to receive his buckle. David is the only other one of our group to be present to share in my glory, just as I shared in his glory the year previously. Even more important is that I receive my award in front of all the people who have also attempted and succeeded in this event, and that is very important to me. That I can stand there with and before them for even a brief second is an honor that goes beyond words. We are the same warriors who began this battle so many long hours ago, and we represent those who have won the battle; together we have conquered the trail and won the war. We have defeated the enemy as individuals, yet we have crossed the same footsteps together in our pilgrimage, and here at the awards ceremony, we honor each other.

Picking up the Silver Buckle and finisher's jacket at the awards ceremony.

After the winners and top placers are brought forward and given their trophies and cash awards, each finisher is called in the order of finish to receive his or her appropriate award. The under 24 hour finishers receive their belt buckles and finisher jackets. One by one we file up to the awards table as our names are announced, a single file line in reverse order as we finished the race. It takes only a brief moment to pick up our awards, but that moment remains forever imbedded in my consciousness. I clutch my silver belt buckle firmly, feel its heavy weight, and smile inside with delight. Forever, it will be a symbolic part of my quest for the end of the trail.

What is it that makes this buckle so important? The Western States silver buckle is one of the most significant awards I've ever encountered in all of sports. This award is given to all runners who finish the race in under 24 hours, a task that only 96 out of the 415 starters accomplished on that particular day.

The buckle is a beautiful piece of art and something that a runner can rightly be proud of having and displaying. Obviously it has a high monetary value, but it is really worthless except to the runner who has earned it. It is very heavy and made of solid sterling silver with an inlaid gold-plated runner surrounded by a mountain scene in the background. On the buckle are the words, "100 Miles, One Day: Western States Endurance Run." On the back of the buckle is the runner's name and his official time. The engraving is done after the end of the race and before the awards ceremony. To me the heaviness of the buckle is also symbolic, maybe representing the heaviness of the task that it took to earn it.

Many runners have gained a collections of buckles, but I'm sure that even to them the first one earned is the most significant. I may never again experience getting another one, but the one I have is very special. No one will ever be able to take it away from me; no matter what my future in running, for one day in one year I earned myself this special award. This feeling is probably prevalent among the majority of us so-called average runners who are fortunate to have one great day. It is perhaps the most sought after award in all ultra endurance sports.

Getting my first buckle in my first try is something that I dare to dream about, but I also know that to achieve any difficult and worthwhile goal, it takes hard work, and my faith in being successful is based entirely on my physical and mental training months before the race. I appreciate all the friends who help me earn the award, but I also know that when it comes down to crunch time and the race is in progress during the last few hours, there is only one person responsible for the outcome. No one can help me make it to that finish line except my own determination and courage.

Even for the first week or so after I receive my buckle, I sometimes have to convince myself that it has really happened, that I am not still dreaming. As an individual who possesses that buckle, I do feel differently, although I like to think that basically I haven't really changed that much. The strength of the buckle gives me a small edge of an inner power that I never have had previously. It is the power of confidence that I can overcome almost any obstacle because I am one of those who have done it successfully in my race. I may never run another mile, but I know that on that one particular day I was able to overcome giant obstacles and accomplish something that few mortals can ever dream of doing. The buckle is part of my personality now, forever etching its influence on my attitude and perspective on life.

I have confidence because I know that there can be very few tougher situations than the one I encounter and successfully conquer. The buckle reminds me that I can go out and prepare myself to handle any situation that I need or want to handle. I don't feel as many fears as I did before doing this race, because I have already faced a tremendous fear previous to the race by putting myself on the line. If I fail or succeed, everyone will know about it; I have no place to hide. The spotlight is on my preparation, my will, my courage or lack of it to continue the brutal journey to the finish line.

I enjoy wearing the buckle, one of the reasons being that it is a great addition to one's wardrobe. It looks nice on a nice belt; anyway, there just seems no reason to put it on display somewhere where no one will notice it. Now I never think twice about having it on; I do get a lot of questions about it from running and non-running friends alike. Sometimes I feel that I might be showing it off too much, but a close running friend of mine who is an excellent runner says that wearing it or showing it to people is not showing off if I really have earned it. Often I am tempted to put the buckle away for special occasions and not look at it or wear it for a long time because it does seem like a means of seeking flattery.

Sometimes it is almost embarrassing to wear it in front of others, especially non-runners, because they do not really understand its importance, its attachment to my innermost emotions. Yet when I do wear it, it becomes a natural part of my dress, attaching itself and its unseeing power tightly to my heart and mind. I feel like it holds a hidden power, like Aladdin's magic lamp. I might rub it and gain the power of all my wishes.

Looking back I remember for a couple of years before I did the race seeing some other runners showing off their buckles, and I didn't ever feel that they were really showing off. To me I felt they had every right and privilege to display their buckles, and I was somewhat in awe of them. Showing off these buckles actually became an inspiration for me to try to earn one, although at the time I believed only a superhuman physical and mental being could possibly ever win one. Perhaps my own buckle will inspire another runner to earn one for himself. I could dare ask for more in my ultrarunning.

The slowly dripping sands of minutes, hours, days, and years have continued on their inevitable journey downward on some endless path, and time has somehow extended some twenty years beyond that first inspiration of the silver belt buckle. I am no longer the eager runner ready for the challenges of the trails. The body is much older now and certainly nowhere near the same physical condition and with the same capacity of conquering such a mammoth race. In fact, my abilities to challenge any trails with any speed at all is forever gone. Yet despite this somewhat grim fact of growing older, the belt buckle still retains its place on a shelf in a prominent place in my living room.

However, I rarely think about the buckle anymore. In fact, sometimes months go by between glances at it by me or anyone else. Suddenly I encounter it in some rare moment when I might be dusting the shelf and have to move the buckle and other items on display out of the way. Being silver, the silver no longer glows brightly but has faded over into a dark green color as untreated silver will tend to do. Only then I pull out a jar of silver polish and take a few minutes to brighten it up once again and replace it on the shelf, knowing that when the next time I notice it, it will be faded again.

I don't wear the buckle anymore. I don't go out of my way to show it to anyone. I almost never tell anyone about it anymore. I have mostly different immediate friends than I had twenty years, although some of my old ex-running friends are still around, and these current friends really don't understand what I once did. Like my running, my buckle is in its place of retirement on the shelf and will probably remain in peace and repose for as long I live. I no longer have the desire to bring it out as a topic of discussion unless someone asks about it.

I can go weeks without even thinking about what happened all those long years ago, but once in a while the memory creeps back up and reminds me what I did then and what I can continue to do now but in different venues. It reminds me that it takes courage to be unique and daring, to take a chance, maybe to fail for everyone to see but also to succeed in some aspect of life that is unexpected. The symbolic nature of the buckle will never go away from my psyche.

It almost seems sad that the buckle has taken a back seat to my life, but that is how it should be. I have found that living in the past all the time is a futile way to take the journey to the end of the trail of one's life. As for that memorable race many years ago, I must leave it and the buckle behind me and forge forward through the jungles of life's challenges on new trails and new adventures.

CHAPTER 17
TAKING CARE OF THE BODY

In today's era of ultrarunning correct care of the body prior to and during a long race has become the subject of many studies. Also, runners of all kinds want the important edge that nutrition provides during the race in order to finish in good shape. Some observations I made about such topics immediately after my race 20 years ago indicate that not much is really very new from then to now. People make new studies but the same conclusions are usually drawn.

In a race of this nature, special considerations must be made for an endurance event well past what is considered average. Running the Western States successfully involves carrying many of my survival supplies with me as I run the course. That means I must have these items in my actual physical presence every step of the way. Whether I take only one bottle filled with liquid or carry a waist pack of some kind, it is virtually impossible to survive without some kind of kit. There are 24 different stops along the run, which is adequate during normal circumstances to insure the runner plenty of help, but sometimes even all these stops aren't enough to give enough help on certain sections between some of the stops.

I must contend often with five or six mile stretches of extreme heat and dust with severe uphills and downhills, all situations which may mean that I might need extra water or some kind of liquid. There may also be that unexpected moment out there on the trail when some type of emergency may occur when a first aid kit of some kind is needed. Night running requires that even more precious supplies be carried.

There are endless different kinds of packs that I might carry with me during the race, just as there are endless kinds of running shoes. Each runner decides what he or she needs and what kind of carrier is the most comfortable. Just as with shoes, no one kind of carrier is the most comfortable; the best one depends on what fits the runner. Before selecting the best one for myself, I try out several kinds and look at many others. Even then I am still not sure I have picked the best one. The extra weight of the pack can take its toll over a hundred miles, so the lighter it is, the better. Those few extra ounces add up quickly after 24 hours of intense running. I always find that I tend to take too much with me in the way of supplies, but those certain emergencies may arise on the trail when I will be sorry I didn't take enough.

On example concerns my flashlights. I carry with me a solid high intensity, slightly heavy light with two D batteries. I have plenty of extra batteries with me, but decide to clip on to my pack an extra, small flashlight in case something happens to my big one. Now I have never had a bulb go out on a flashlight, especially a new one, but that is what happens when I change batteries for the first time. I am glad for that extra light which works beautifully for me for an eight mile stretch. If I do the race again, I will take an extra bulb. Despite all my planning, for some reason I forgot to do so. It is also tricky trying to decide how many batteries I might need, and where I can drop off extra batteries in a drop bag at an aid station. It is safer to have too many batteries than to try to run in the dark or with one light between the racer and his pacer.

During the first half of the Western States I carry two bottles on my pack and one in my hand. Later on I find that the two 16 ounce bottles are enough so I drop the one I carry in my hand off with my crew at the next access. I have a small pocket on my pack where I carry a mini first aid kit of mole skin, bandages, aspirin, and several other items. I also carry some biodegradable toilet paper, a few tidbits of salty food items, and a scarf, which can be used in several kinds of emergencies.

Packs can jiggle if put on loosely or if they don't fit correctly. I tighten mine securely at the beginning of the run and it fits nicely. Usually after running for a while I have to tighten it again, but if I am hydrating enough to keep my weight up, I have a slightly bloated feeling and my pack doesn't need adjusting. Several things must be taken in consideration in choosing a pack. The pack must be able to ride securely if the runner has a bouncing stride; the size of the pockets must be considered if the runner wishes to take extra items; the pack must be able to ride comfortably on the runner who has a bigger or a small buttock than the average runner. The runner should check all of this out well before race day arrives.

The six miles between Michigan Bluff and Foresthill I carry two water bottles, and give my pack to my crew for two reasons. First it gives my hips and back a short break, and the relief feels wonderful. Second, it gives my crew time to prepare the pack with my night supplies. I show them well before the race what I want in my pack for the night portion, and they then give the pack back to me before I enter the canyon and begin my night running. I find those few miles I don't have to wear any pack is a tremendous relief and recovery for my hips and back.

During the night I add two small pockets to my pack for carrying extra batteries and my extra flashlight. In addition I have batteries and a light windbreaker waiting for me in one of my drop bags at a night aid station. Once the runner reaches the last few miles of the race, the pack can probably be dropped off again with the crew and the bottles can be carried. I believe it is very critical to have something to cut down the cooling effect of the night air after the runner crosses the river. I have a light jacket that can be stuffed into a pack pocket, but I end up wearing it all the way to the finish line.

Do things ever go wrong with the pack or transferring items in or out? We all get in a hurry sometimes, especially when we are under some kind of stress and want something immediately. Twice I am careless in

A large group gets ready to take a practice run over the first 30 miles of the course.

replacing my bottles back on my pack and they fall off, both times while I am running or walking. One time the bottle drops over a bank and comes to rest against a tree stump about five feet below the trail. It is night and I am with my pacer at the time. While I shine a light at the bottle, he scrambles down and retrieves it, not without some difficulty.

My pacer also has a problem as one of his bottles goes flying down the bank at night never to be seen again. Fortunately he has an extra one that is almost full of water to get him to the next aid station. Another time he discovers he has forgotten to close one of his pockets and finds that several batteries have apparently bounced out of the pocket and are gone somewhere down a bank in the middle of the night. Transferring items to and from the pack can also be a problem, and I often find myself half twisting the pack so I can see what I am getting. Dropping or losing important items show the necessity for carrying backup items or at least having them available at the next drop station or with my crew at the next crew access point.

While walking up one steep, three mile hill I find it more convenient and comfortable to completely turn the pack around with everything in front of me for awhile. Also I utilize the uphill walking sessions to take care of most of my heavy drinking and eating needs. Gulping down huge quantities of liquid is difficult at best while running down a fast hill, at the same time peeking with one eye around the bottle to avoid a pratfall.

One other disaster almost strikes. After changing to the emergency flashlight, my pacer and I leave an aid station. The only extra batteries for the flashlight are in a small pocket attached to my pack. About 50 yards out I discover it has come off during the rest at the aid station. My pacer hurries back to find it, while I take off running. Just over five minutes later he catches up with me, fortunately with the extra batteries. I play a mental game at the time trying to see how hard I can run for how long a time to keep ahead of him.

At each station I grab a small handful of pretzels or crackers to take with me to eat after leaving the station. One problem with this type of food is that it seems to take forever to chew and swallow, and I become impatient. I usually put a few in my pack for later use, often because I can't eat all of it at that time, and I don't know what to do with the extra food. Two days after the race when I clean out my pack, I find the bottom of one pocket littered with broken pretzels and smashed crackers. I am like a squirrel who never has gotten back to his stash.

Carrying backpacks with supplies is common for ultrarunners and if not done with common sense and the runner's comfort in mind, can become a nuisance. I work with these problems on practice runs well before the race. Like any good stage play, the details of performing on the Western States Trail must be rehearsed over and over again before the live performance.

Another concern I have on this run, which I feel is at least one third percent of successfully completing the race, is the consumption of food and liquids during the event. I have experienced the wall in a marathon when my glycogen stores have been used up. It is an agonizing moment for any marathoner.

There can be no wall on this 100 miler. My tempo will greatly avoid that, but also I must replace my glycogen stores and keep myself hydrated throughout by eating and drinking on the run, often times to the point where I feel slightly uncomfortable. I can't just do it on race day for the very first time. For months on long practice runs, I drink and eat and drink some more, experimenting with many different kinds of liquids and solids my own stomach can digest comfortably. I condition my stomach, much as I condition my legs, to meet the demands and stresses it will face on the trail. I train my entire system to this refueling activity for months before the race. Often I eat lightly and purposefully and then go for a run right away without the usual time to let the food digest. If I get stomach cramps I slow down and walk awhile before trying to run again.

For several months before the race I try just about everything I can possibly find to eat. I finally settle on a few basic items for the race including bananas, cantaloupes, a blended fruit-yogurt mix, cookies, and salted items such as chips, saltines, and pretzels. I also have chicken and vegetable soup ready. I end up by eating not even half the food I have available.

One thing I learn from pacing the previous year and something I discover while training for the race is that there is enough food at the aid stations and enough aid stations available to feed an army. A runner probably can run the entire race without a crew if it becomes necessary. Just about every kind of tasty food is available somewhere. All that food I leave with my crew is probably not needed, but it is comfortable knowing I have food of my own choice available. Even then I know I have prepared too much food, that there is no way I'm going to eat all of it.

All of these facts I realize ahead of time, yet I am still over prepared. So what really happens, of course, is exactly what I know will happen. I eat only a fraction of the prepared food and the aid station food is definitely enough both in taste and volume. During the first three stops with my crew I do eat some of the prepared food, but I really don't consume very much, certainly much less than I think I do. I also eat rather sparingly at the aid stations. The only food I really force myself to eat are the salty items, so I won't become sodium diluted with all the liquid I am drinking.

Every time I run an ultra I find it difficult to eat effectively. For one thing it takes time to eat, and I don't have enough time to really chew very much food properly. As I stuff it into my mouth, my mouth becomes full, and then I can't get it down fast enough. What I end up doing is washing it down with water and cutting my eating short. For me my fruit-blended mix and cantaloupe go down the easiest. I know I should take more time to eat properly but I never do.

Another thing that happens to me is that at about 40 miles as the afternoon sun begins to beat down more intensely and warm up the canyons, I lose my appetite. I just don't feel like eating at all. One experienced runner I run with for awhile during the race tells me not to fight it; he says that it is difficult to digest food when it's hot, so just go along with the feeling and don't eat, but drink a lot of fluids instead. It sounds like solid advice; I try it and it seems to work well with me.

I continue to not feel hungry as the race continues into the dark night hours. One thing I do is to continue to force into my stomach the salty items, which I have to jam down my throat because they begin to taste awful. Sometimes I even carry them with me to eat at some point when I have to walk for a little while. The only other food I take in after dark is hot soup. I eat and drink a cup at several different aid stations. Each cup might be a different flavor, but the taste is satisfying, the soup is easy to swallow, and the warmth settles my stomach. Some of it is almost too hot so I have to blow and sip. One important thing about the soup is that it contains a good quantity of salt. I had not used soup very much on my training runs, but now it is definitely on my list for night running. I believe I will probably consume it cold if that is the only way it is prepared.

During the entire run I consume probably enough food to constitute one good lunch meal, certainly not much more than that. It appears hardly enough in calories or carbohydrates to keep me refueled for 100 miles, yet

I seem to make out all right without losing much general energy. What keeps me going then? I have no reliable way to prove the true reason, but I believe that it must be in part to a high calory, glycogen replacement drink that I consume for most of the race. I use it during my 50 mile runs and always feel strong at the end of those races.

I am not plugging any drink or food item over any other; there are many different items on the market that can do the job. I just happen to select one of several drinks that ultrarunners often use in these races. I actually only have it put in two of my bottles when I have access to my crew. At the regular aid stations I take only water, and I always have one bottle of water with me even when I have the other drink. Also at the aid stations I sip various other drinks, including soft drinks, that are provided. Probably over two thirds of what I drink is just plain water. Apparently I consumed a lot of my special drink, according to my crew.

Just as my taste for food leaves me, the special drink begins to taste terrible to me during the later stages of the race. The last time I fill my bottles with it is at the river crossing, still with a long 22 miles left in the race. To me it has a rather weak, punch-like taste, and as the day wears on, I have my crew dilute it even further to get rid of as much of the taste as possible. As I say, I have no proof, but I truly believe it does provide me with glycogen stores that help my muscles work to get me to the finish line. One positive thing it does for sure is to convince my body and mind that it does work.

My favorite drink is just plain water. It is basically tasteless, goes down easily, is plentiful at each aid station, and keeps my body from dehydrating. I drink it all during the day and night, and often literally force enormous quantities into my stomach even when I don't feel thirsty. If I feel the least bit thirsty at all, I know I'm not drinking enough. Early in the race it seems I must urinate about every ten to fifteen minutes, and it sometimes becomes a nuisance to have to stop so often; however, I realize the delays become money in the bank later on in the race. Even during the last stages of the run, I must stop about every 30 or 40 minutes to relieve myself. My stomach sometimes sloshes loudly enough to be heard, and I often run with that bloated feeling, but the discomfort tells me I am well hydrated. My weight is always up at the medical checks, and this fact is a confidence boost that I must be doing something correctly.

Later on when I pick up my pacer, I tell him to periodically remind me to drink, as in my fatigue I sometimes simply forget to do so. Even by that time water is getting to taste awful. Drinking water constantly for almost 24 hours gives it an unpalatable taste after awhile, even though it has no true taste. The other great advantage of water is that I can pour it on myself to cool off during the heat of the day.

Much is made of drinking the water from free flowing streams because of possible contamination. The only water I use is the icy cold, fast flowing snow melt from the higher altitudes. I do that only twice. The rest of the race I use only what is available at the aid stations. I use all the streams I find for another purpose, however. I throw water over my head and wet my cap and bandanna before putting them back on. The cold water refreshes me and helps keep my body and skin temperature down. It makes me more comfortable, helps keep me from overheating, and makes it easier for me to move faster with more energy. Basically I use the stream water to put on my body; I use the aid station water to put in my body. There is plenty of both available. However, if I would have found myself dehydrated and out of water, I would have drunk the stream water and worried about the consequences later.

What I do learn from my experience dealing with nourishment is that each runner is different. The individual runner must decide what will work best for him or her and be ready to make necessary adjustments during the course of the race. The important thing to realize is that food and fluid intake is a necessary and important element to succeed in this race. It is part of the total aspect of body management and must be done with a conscious and thorough effort in order to finish the 100 miles.

I slowly stretch my left leg under the sheets feeling the familiar tug of stiffness that comes with each new morning. My leg now straightens as I pull back the covers and gradually inch my way into a standing position and take a few cautious and light-treaded steps across the carpet. The dull throbbing pushes against my mind, only a small annoyance in my daily preparation for this day's activities.

For five months prior to the running of the Western States my knee begins each day the same way, the dull stiffness on the inside, a pinpointed spot that almost feels like a bruise. Within a few minutes of moving about and putting pressure on it, the pain almost disappears completely, and I totally forget about it while involved in my activities. Only again in the evening when I sit down and then try to move it, does the stiffness come back.

Each day when I go for a run, be it a five or fifty miler, the pain subsides after a couple of hundred yards, never to appear again for the duration of the run. My mind plays mental tricks. I ask myself what might be wrong, yet the injury seems to be oblivious to my running, only reoccurring during inactivity. I use ice and it helps to ease the stiffness somewhat, but it still remains and in fact increases with increased mileage as race day gets closer. With a month to go the stiffness even begins to creep in during my training runs, but I continue on and the pain is only a minor inconvenience. Sometimes it even creeps in right during the middle of a long training run.

Even resting several days before the big race doesn't seem to help. The day before the race I cover the spot with a bag of ice whenever I have a spare moment, hoping against hope that the stiffness and pain will go away. Only my mind tells me that if form holds true, the pain will disappear as it always does once I begin to run. My mind tells me this fact, but a little voice in the background keeps telling me that I have never done 100 miles before and that my knee can't possibly hold up for that long. All I can do is have faith and go out and run as long as I am able. The same pain was there before each previous race, and the pain disappeared then and never returned. I must feel in my attitude that it will go away and never return during this race also. I realize that at this date I can't do anything about the situation anyway.

Race morning arrives and the stiffness is barely noticeable. I prepare for the race, go through the warmups and preliminaries, and the race begins. The emotion of the event envelops me completely, and I run the 100 miles to Auburn. Not only does my knee not bother me, but I never think about it once from the moment after I get up that morning until some time the day after I finish the race. Ironically the knee doesn't flare up again for four days. Then it is moderately stiff for a couple of weeks, but no worse than before the race. As I cut my training mileage back to 40 a week, within a month the stiffness virtually disappears.

The point of this story is to illustrate that injuries are part of an athlete's life, and certainly a major area of concern for the ultrarunner who may train 80 to 100 miles a week as I do for this event. The injury nags and says to slow down; the mind says to keep training hard; the heart says to compromise, to ease off and find the right point in the middle. The tugs of pressure to do well in the race, countered by the pain and debilitating effects of the injury, are constant worries for those of us who train for such events.

With my own injuries I follow a training philosophy of listening to my body carefully and then trying to cut a fine edge of training to match my aches and pains. I train according to how my body feels and as long as the injury doesn't affect my training, I deny it exists. I really don't want to know what my injury is or what the cause is; if the only solution is to back off in my running, I will not do it as long as I can go on comfortably. As long as the injury is under control, I want no doctor to tell me to stop. I feel that only my body can tell me that, and if the pain is severe enough I will stop running.

Ultrarunners are not ordinary runners who follow normal judgments of what a long or short distance training run consists of. A ten mile run may be a gigantic distance for the average runner training for a 10K, but for me it may be a light workout thrown in between my long weekend workouts of 30 miles on back to back days. Just as I know when I am doing a workout what my pace is, I must know just how much my body will tolerate and not become injured. I deal with potential injuries by not being over fanatical about my mileage, although my friends may disagree, of being a judge when I am tired and potentially open for injury. I must listen to my finely tuned body, and if I hear some discordant note, I must back off and re-tune myself before continuing.

Trail management of the body; proper diet on the run; awareness and treatment of injuries: taking care of my body is an extremely crucial element I must deal with if I expect to complete my 100 mile adventure.

Today as I look back on my 20 year old training logs, I wonder if all that running didn't somehow contribute to my inability to run anything more than a short jog today. At times my aging body feels like it just doesn't want to get up and move because of the various aches and pains that spring up whenever I put stress on it. Did I somehow wear down my body over all those years with excessive running? There really is no scientific proof that such is what happens to older runners. So why can't I even approach what I did years ago?

I see now that all my running friends go through the same changes. So do my non-running friends. My condition is part of what some call getting older, when the physical capabilities begin to slow down. What I am learning, however, in the realm of my age division, I am still at the same spot I was 20 years ago. I can still do many physical things that my peers only wish they could do.

When I take a long hike across the mountains, I see very few 60-year-old people on the trail. When I do see them they are much slower than I am. When I ski five days in row on often fairly challenging terrain, I do see other people my age, but I find that I can ski harder and longer than only a handful of them. It is much more difficult to fly fish a rock-strewn river than it used to be, and I may need more recovery time, but soon I am back out on that river again.

I know I will never see a 100 miler again; or a 50 miler; or a marathon. However, I might still see a 2 miler, a 5K, or a 10K, and I will go out and plod on down the road or trail in happiness at my old 100 mile pace for the shorter distances. Time is no longer an issue; getting to the finish line is, just as the goal used to be to reach the finish line in the longer races. My shorter races have become my ultras. Let the younger, faster, and newer runners bask in their glory. I have long ago had all the glory I need in life. For me just arriving at the finish line is all the personal fame I need.

CHAPTER 18
TRAINING FOR THE WESTERN STATES

Taking on the challenge of the Western States or any other long ultra event demands a training philosophy, one that is both demanding and flexible, one that emphasizes those areas that the runner will encounter and must overcome on the race course itself. This philosophy needs to fit the individual runner, his strengths and weaknesses, and the amount of time available to prepare for the event.

First of all, let me make it clear that I am not an expert on proper training.

The author with his father and mother on a hike on Mt. Shasta during the summer of 1988.

I have no background in the physical aspects or formal techniques that the many experts have expounded over the many years. Looking back at my training for this race, I can say that not much has really changed in the past 20 years. Certainly much more is known about the body and training methods, nutrition and diet, and the mental aspects of such preparation.

However, as an experiment of one 20 years ago, I basically was my own coach and learned on the run so to speak. This is the advice as I so clearly put it down from the many notes I took at the time just after completing the race. If a runner of average means can get anything out it, I hope it can provide a value to that runner. Here then is what I wrote down about my training from 20 years ago, way back in 1986.

I listen to and read the philosophies of many other runners who have done the race successfully. I take what I can use for myself and look closely at those ideas that I find are not sound for my personal situation. Some runners claim to be able to finish under 24 hours on a minimum amount of mileage, such as 35 or 40 miles per week; if I follow this philosophy I will never make it to the halfway point of the course. I experiment with hill training, different food and drink and every other possible means of running and training. What I come up with works for me; I learn that absolute principles of training can't be found; each person has a different physical makeup that requires an individual program. What I come up with works for me, a very average runner of fairly good size. I follow a regiment that allows me the chance to win the buckle. What follows is simply my opinion, an opinion based upon one person's success.

First, let me deal with mileage. For the six months prior to the race, I run over 2,000 miles, including 400 miles in May, my biggest month of training. Getting out and putting in those 80, 90, and 100 mile weeks is important to my preparation. Speed is not the most important aspect. Simply getting out on the roads and trails and moving for three to six hours at a time, often for several days in a row, becomes a trademark for toughening my body and mind for the long journey I am about to face.

Those who claim the race can be done on normal mileage give false hopes to the vast majority of less talented runners who try to follow that regiment, although I admire those who can back up their claims. I meet many competitors during my training, and among those who fail, one of the major reasons they feel that causes their failures, is not putting in enough miles of training to be able to withstand the almost catastrophic, brutal punishment their bodies receive during the event. Those who do make it on limited mileage are special athletes. However, they are not average ability people; one wonders what they could really do on double or triple the mileage.

Although high mileage is critical to my success, it is tempered by years of an already high mileage base and by a slow, gradual increase over several months. The mileage doesn't become an end in itself; I use it as a gauge to check on my overall training. In fact, about every third or fourth week, I back off slightly maybe 20 miles to recharge my legs and then burst forward again to reach new heights.

Due to necessity, most of my training mileage until April is done on flat terrain. From April onward I begin spending much of my time running the hills. First I begin taking one training run per week on hilly terrain. I then advance to two days a week, and finally I try to run three to four days each week. During the last month before the race, I have an opportunity to run entirely on the hills every day during my training.

The race course itself is one hill after another, and I believe one of the keys to making it to the finish and completing the course in under 24 hours is being able to take off with confidence and run hard on the downhills, knowing the legs will hold up and recover on the uphills. The other main key is to have the patience and skill to walk all uphills that hold any kind of steepness at all, running those uphill sections that are gradual and rolling. I constantly train on hills by running hard downhill, strengthening the appropriate muscles, and walking fast uphill, training that is almost opposite and contrary to all advised training techniques.

Let me explain my reasoning. Normal running mentality for this race must be adjusted. This race does not traverse a normal course. If I hope to be successful, I must faithfully practice very hard what the course demands that I do. The circuit demands that legs be totally fit and hardened to run the steep, long mileage sections of downhill trails. The runner must prepare by running the same way as in a rehearsal. I have a steep three mile hill 15 miles from my home, and I spend countless after work hours in the middle of the week walking and jogging to the top, catching my breath, and then blasting hard to the bottom, pain often jarring through my quads, begging me to slow down. I reach the bottom, take a break, and repeat the run: 12 tough, race-preparing miles.

The hills must become second nature to the Western States runner. The legs must be battle toughened, ready to take on any steepness, anytime during the 100 miles. I believe I relish the downhills because my legs are ready for them. These hills are my strength, and while many others might dread them, I anticipate them with an inner delight, because I have made them an asset. Certainly I still receive the pain that comes with the tremendous forces on my lower extremities, but I recover quickly on the move because my body has practiced it over and over again a countless number of hours and days making the hills my friends.

Almost as crucial as the running of the downhills is the walking of the uphills. Except for the gentle uphills, only a fool runs the uphills, only to suffer later by having to drop out because of fatigue. Most runners don't practice walking, and I admit to not being a fast walker, but I do try to develop a comfortable uphill technique that will allow me to recover. If I were to do the race again, that is the one area where I would put in more time, developing a quicker walking style.

Long training runs every weekend present some problems in terms of boredom and finding time to run all day. I determine from the very beginning two basic tenets of my weekend long outings in preparation for the race. I mix in using back to back Saturday/Sunday runs of between 20 and 30 miles each run and use marathons and 50 mile races as training runs for the Western States. I do one of the two routines almost every weekend for the four months before the race. I also participate in three of the organized training runs on the race trail itself, which I will discuss later.

First, let me address the back to back runs. I feel that I will simply destroy myself if I try for 50 to 70 mile runs all of the time. I find that frequent 25-30 milers give me the endurance base I need without wearing me out, while the back to back long runs improve my body's ability to recover quickly. My body becomes accustomed to the high mileage but not all in one big swoop. I have something remaining for race day.

Racing is a challenge any time and also a lot more interesting than simply taking a long training run. Therefore I use various marathons and 50 mile races as training in preparation for the 100 miler. Most of these races I back my pace off slightly and don't run them all out. By going a little slower than normal, I am able to conserve myself, thus leading to a quicker recovery. I am able to resume my regular training almost immediately. During the four and a half months before the race, I complete three marathons, a 12 hour run, and three 50 milers.

I first run a marathon in February, cruising in with a 3:36. I follow this race by doing the windy and rainy Jedediah Smith 50 with a qualifying time of 8:38. This also comes soon after I had been very ill with a viral infection. Even though the conditions were all against me, this time is still my fastest 50 mile time before the 100 miler.

In March I do another marathon, running a fairly hard 3:14. I follow this one week later with a 12 hour track run, logging just under 65 miles, which turns out to be my longest continuous run before the big race. At the end of both races, I am encouraged because I still feel very strong. The 65 miles provides me with a boost of confidence because it is well beyond the half way distance of the race, and I still feel reasonably strong.

My big race in April is the American River 50, where I plan to run a fast time, but instead hold back for a slow 8:52. However, I am back running strongly the very next day. I also throw in two 10K races and a hilly eight mile race.

In May I begin with the very tough Wild, Wild West Marathon, a hilly cross country run, and run it fairly hard for a respectable 3:46. This effort takes one day of recovery time before I can really run again. Finally four weeks before the race I do the difficult Nugget 50. My pacer and I run the entire race together in a slow, conservative 10:17, but we get a touch of the types of hills in the upcoming race. I feel strong at the end and only half expended, so we both get up the next day and run a local 10K hilly road race.

Every race with perhaps of the exception of the Wild, Wild West Marathon, I run much less than all out, trying to get a feel for pace and working hard to finish each race strongly, which I am able to accomplish. At the end of each race, if someone had said I had to do five more miles, I could have done them. The last 50 miler I was particularly cautious not to blow up and leave my Western States race out on the course.

Does this regiment of races work? It works for me, it seems, but each runner should do what he or she feels is best for the individual. Running those long training runs on the trails and hills, and combining them with marathons and other ultra events as preparation, seems to be a viable way to train for the Western States. One other side advantage that a race has over a training run is the lack of boredom. The runner is more motivated in a race than during a training run that has only the motivation of just finishing. It's difficult to do a 50 mile training run, but not so bad doing a 50 mile race.

Another aspect to my training is doing many long practice runs on trails.

I constantly use the many and varied trails of the nearby southern Sierras in Sequoia National Park for my weekend training workouts. Several of us often go together, stop along the way to enjoy the scenery and rest, and simply make the entire day a satisfying adventure. Time is not important here; getting used to running trails decisively and comfortably is the main purpose. I base my training on the hours spent moving in some way, whether slow or fast. Mileage and pace are difficult to determine anyway out here on the trails because of the constant changing conditions of the trails and the pitch of the terrain.

The main objective of these outings is to establish credibility as a trail runner, to know how to handle all the aspects of the trail that will be encountered on the Western States, to shift one's running mentality to that of the patient, unhurried runner who now runs as naturally on the trails as on the roads. It requires a different discipline from the roads, one of being able to negotiate all the hundreds of various combinations of dirt, limbs, rocks, pitch, and other unseen parts that go into the makeup of such a long, diversified surface. Gone is the sameness of the road; present is the infinite variety and surprises of this new route. The successful finisher must practice to make it a complete part of his running experience.

One last, but I believe, important aspect of trail running practice is to enjoy the experience. Running with friends, stopping at streams, walking up the hills, yelling in the deep, darkened woods: all of this should be fun. The run has a training purpose but enjoying the outing should be a primary function of the training.

One of my favorite areas to run is in Sequoia National Park, only about 30 or so miles from where I live in Visalia, California, a city of over 100,000 people located in the heart of the San Joaquin Valley about 40 miles south of Fresno. The park offers a variety of different trails, high altitude, and plenty of snow before it melts in the early spring. It also offers outstanding scenery. The trails are well maintained and marked, and it is difficult to get lost on them. A group of six of us, including three running the Western States, one day run about 11 miles out and back on the High Sierra Trail during mid-spring. We go as far as we can before losing the trail in the snow. We run, walk the hills, walk and jog over both snow patches and deep snow until we can no longer locate the trail.

I am in no big hurry on these training runs. I may take a stretch of 30 minutes and run fairly hard to test myself, then back off a little to enjoy the scenery. I love to stop at a stream and cool myself off and even sit down to rest. Running with others, we run as one group, as pairs or threes, and occasionally alone, but we usually stop once every few miles to wait for everyone to catch up. The joy of these runs is that it is not a race, not a time to be a hero.

I try to learn several things on these runs. First, I work on getting the "feel" of running on trails, the constant changing of ups and downs, the switching from a good section to a bad section, the learning to concentrate on every step. Speed here is often not important to me. I am not keeping a clock or measuring how far I have gone. I also work on the specificity of the race. I will take off and charge down a hill to get my legs ready for the downhill racing sections. I will stop and walk as quickly as I can up a hill for the same reason. However, I won't do this on every hill, just once in a while. The rest of the time I will work on my steady pacing, trying to run free of any strain and pain, just comfortable enough to enjoy the run and feel reasonably well by the end of the day.

I'll never forget that one day three of us take off on a gentle up and back section of 12 miles on a lesser used park trail that had everything from open running to brush covering the surface. On the way back we encounter a nice breeze as we run in a section of shade under some tall trees, the trail covered with old leaves and small limbs. Suddenly all of us are yelling, a yell of abandoned joy I would like to think, as we tear down a gentle downhill section. Our yelling echoes across the mountainside and through the woods, with only our own ears hearing the shouts. I wonder what anyone hiking up the trail might think of us, probably that we have just escaped from some nuthouse up high in the mountains. We run relaxed and at a strong pace, but we truly have fun.

Another of my favorite places to run is in the northern part of the state near the Oregon border, on the Pacific Crest Trail where it crosses Interstate 5. Several times during a two week period just three weeks before the race, I run up the mountainside 10 or 11 miles on one side of the freeway and then turn around and run back down. Three days later I repeat the run on the other side of the highway. It gives me all hills and a wide variety of trail conditions. After those sessions I feel I am finally tuned up for the race.

In training for the race, all the aspects that may be encountered should be practiced and rehearsed ahead of time in an attempt to feel comfortable and especially not to be surprised when encountering a new situation.

I place running in the heat a top priority. The runner who heat trains, practicing the intake of fluids, will be ready to meet the searing canyon temperatures at least on a survival level. Runners cannot go into the race hoping the heat won't be a factor; it might be cool for awhile, but that heat training will take away the surprise when one suddenly encounters the inevitable 100 degree canyons 60 miles into the race.

Pacing practice is important as a part of the overall training. Thinking about mileage time, one has to average just over 14 minutes per mile to complete the course in under 24 hours. Some of us if we push the pace on the flat, can do that while walking. Yet we all know that walking the entire course under 24 hours is impossible. How many of us ever take our training workouts at or slower than a 14 minute per mile pace? Probably none of us do it. We always go faster than that, even when we crank our pace way down.

Yet, when we train for a 10K, the only time we go at a faster than race pace is during our weekly track and speed workouts. Otherwise we always run at under race pace. Yet for the 100 miler we always train faster than race pace. It does seem to make sense to go slower, but we know that such a practice pace would go so very slowly that we may not make any physical gains. Perhaps putting on a light pack and jogging and walking through the mountains for eight hours and covering 30 miles or more might seem like anything but beneficial, but wouldn't it be an approximate race pace? Certainly it would be low key and enjoyable.

The distance done slowly gives me a sense of mental patience and physical strength. The power of the legs to move for endless hours is developed. My body recovers quickly, ready for another test the very next day. Most of all the workout becomes a happy adventure, a time to play with the trail and the body, an opportunity to engage in blissful mind games, like counting how many switchbacks there are on a section of trail or powering aggressively up one particularly tough section.

One final aspect of my training philosophy deals with taking practice runs on the trail itself. Each of the runs is done in a group setting, designed specifically as preparation for the race. I always go with a group of runners who are a little slower than myself. I stop frequently, ask constant questions, probing the minds of experienced runners, constantly developing in my mind pictures of different sections of the Western States trail.

My goal on these runs is not just to improve my conditioning but to get to know the trail itself. On these runs I am content to not be in any hurry at all, although I do part of the section from Robinson Flat to Michigan Bluff rather hard. Generally I want to enjoy the run, look at the scenery and the landmarks, and get a feel for and memorize the trail so I will know where I am on race day. On race day I know I won't have time to look around and enjoy everything, so I do it on the training runs instead. I try to memorize every possible detail of the trail that will help me on race day. I learn where I can make up time and where I will lose time, so mentally I won't panic during the race itself.

I find all this knowledge helpful on race day. Some sections are fast sections and some are slow. If I seem to waste some time walking up a steep hill, I won't become impatient and begin to run unnecessarily because I realize that I can make up that time on the next downhill section because from my training run I know what to expect. Because of this knowledge I can comfortably adjust my pace to the trail, and in the end I am able to hold my sub-24 hour cushion just under the line for the entire race and finish it successfully.

Another aspect of the training that is often overlooked is one's general diet and the ideal body weight for the demands of the race. During all the weeks of training I did not rely on any special diet except that I tried to generally eat more nutritious foods than I normally would. With all the calories that I expended during the training I found that I was always hungry and often consumed a great amount of calories. Often those calories weren't the best kinds, but I made a conscious attempt to eat more fruits and vegetables and get plenty of carbohydrates.

As for my weight, an interesting thing happened. My normal weight while running has always been around 185 pounds with a small variance. I'm almost six feet tall, so that seems a little on the heavy side but I feel good at that weight. Because of the vigorous training for this race, I lost a lot of weight and was down to almost 170 pounds for race day. I believe the lower weight was very significant in my making it successfully to the finish line.

As Rob and I glide down the road just a few miles from the finish of the Nugget 50 with four weeks to go, a surge of confidence comes over me. I know with a couple of more weeks of intense hill training, I will be ready for the race.

Twenty years later as I scan over my training logs from 20 years ago, I am amazed that I was able to do that much mileage. For another 10 years I was able to keep up the training with only a small falloff. Then about 10 years ago my strength started to weaken at a fast rate, so that during the last few years I do about 30 slow miles of fast walking and slow jogging a week and that is about all I can handle comfortably.

Two years ago I was slowly gliding along a trail on a narrow ridge top on some mountains near where I grew up as a child. I walked quickly up a hill, then turned to a choppy jog on the down slope, repeating my moves as the terrain shifted from up to down and back to up again. The scenery was terrific, the terrain challenging. Wild flowers bloomed by the thousands in a meadow. A deer crashed though the woods. A rattlesnake even buzzed me from the middle of the trail. The summer breeze would suddenly gust up and waft its cool air through my sweat-soaked hair. It was a fun day as I finally reached the top of the mountain some six miles from the start of the trail. At the top was an abandoned forest service fire lookout station, partially collapsed and totally unusable.

I opened my waist pack and pulled out some snacks and nibbled at them and took some sips on my water bottle. I took in the wide expanse of scenery, a giant canyon spread out before me that dipped 2,000 feet down into the world of civilization below me. I watched a giant freeway snake up the canyon, and I could vaguely make out below me my old home town, a winding river, and the tiny image of a freight train twisting its way down the canyon next to the river.

I can no longer do the long runs I used to do, I thought, but I can still do this. My body has slowed down but it is not busted up yet. Somehow all those long runs years ago played a part of where I am today. Without them I might be sitting in a chair and doing nothing, that is, nothing really worthwhile. As long my physical engine can still chug up the canyon like the twisty old freight train, my body and mind will always find a new, untraveled trail somewhere on the earth where I live.

CHAPTER 19

MIND GAMES

Visualizing the results of an athletic contest is something athletes of all sports strive to do to enhance their performances. They "see" in their minds the events happening certain ways, or they picture themselves relaxed and concentrating and performing at the highest levels possible. It is a technique used in a variety of different ways by many athletes and can be used effectively in non-athletic endeavors also.

I use visualization many, many times before the Western States and even during the race itself. I use it on training runs, picturing myself running smoothly and effortlessly through the woods, up and down long hills without discomfort, my feet barely gliding above the trail surface. Often while I am sitting or lying down resting, I picture myself running. I see myself arriving at certain points along the course with a definite amount of time remaining, each such time within the cushion of finishing under 24 hours. I run the trail itself in training runs and envision the pace I will use, where I will try to make up time and where I will simply resign myself to slowing down and conserving myself. Never in my mind's picture do I see negative happenings. Everything that happens is in a positive vein, but I do visualize myself overcoming tough obstacles like a steep uphill or a section of the trail with stifling, hot afternoon temperatures.

I also make some realistic judgments as to how fast I can cover certain parts of the trail and still remain inside the comfort zone of physical stability. Combining my practical and emotional expectations, I try to realistically visualize the entire race before I run as a race where everything goes perfectly with no injuries or stomach problems, muscles cramps, or blowing out because of depleted energy stores. On a perfect day I see myself finishing between 23 hours and 30 minutes and 23 hours and 45 minutes. I also know that I might have something happen physically to my body that will slow me down. I therefore see myself having to make a stretch drive to barely make the 24 hour cutoff. I visualize myself emotionally pulling myself up and entering the stadium with less than two minutes to spare, dashing madly for the finish and making it just under the bell.

My biggest fear, and I'm sure one of the biggest fears for any runner in this race, is the fear of entering the track under 24 hours but knowing my best sprint won't make it to the finish line before the clock strikes five o'clock. I would rather know way out there on the trail that I'm not going to make it, then gear back and settle for the next goal of under 30 hours. I don't want my hopes dashed just before the finish line. In my visualization I never picture the finish happening this way. My picture of the finish is always positive, never one of failure. I realistically know that I have a good chance of not making it, but I don't let it enter my mind too often. However, mentally I just tell myself that if I can't finish the race in time, I will be satisfied if I have given my very best.

I'm not a psychologist, but I am a coach of team sports, and my experience with visualization is that it has some positive effects, but only if the athlete is physically ready to handle the task. Positive pictures of success without the physical background to attain that success is only asking for disappointment. The visualization process only enhances the physical ability and preparation. I have to have extreme confidence in my months of brutal, physical preparation, or I know that all these mind games will do no good. No matter how much I see myself being successful, having tired, out of shape legs will just never let me reach the finish line. The physical reality will win out over what my mind wants if my body is unprepared to do it.

The strange part about my race is that so many of the mental images I have of the race concerning distances and times come true almost the exact way I imagine them. One thing that I don't and can't visualize very well is the pain one must endure during the race. I only see the parts where I can use my strength to power up and down the hills, always in control. I cannot picture the pain because I have never gone this far before, and I don't know what it might be like. However, my experiences with 50 mile trail races and long training runs on the trails give me some idea of what I might go through. I steel my mind for the worst possible pain, and the result is that nothing surprises me. As bad as the pain becomes at times, it isn't anything worse than the worse possible situation I imagine in my mind.

My visualization before the race, I feel, has a definite positive impact on the outcome. Yet my visualization during the race is just as important. I hear some advice from a veteran runner which is often repeated by other runners, so I know it must be valid. This advice is that one not consider this race a 100 mile race, that one think of it as a race only to the next checkpoint.

Overall as I run, I picture my race as four overall separate long races. My four races are from the beginning to Robinson Flat - 30 miles; Robinson Flat to Michigan Bluff - 25 miles; Michigan Bluff to Rucky Chucky - 23 miles; and Rucky Chucky to the finish - 22 miles. Within each section I break down the race into sub-sections, only working to complete my run successfully to the next aid station or checkpoint. I never try to look past that next point. My overall journey is a long one, but I know where the gas stations and rest stops are, and I will refuel my mind and body at each one of them before proceeding onward.

I don't think of this as a 100 mile race. I think of it as a run to the next aid station. It is only 5.6 miles, 7.5 miles, or whatever the distance may be. My goal is to race to that next destination. What I have already done is in the past, already gone completely from my mind. I zero in doggedly on the current task at hand, to reach my next rendezvous with the aid station personnel, or as the case may be, my crew. I know I can run 5.6 miles, but don't know if I can run 100, so I take the shorter distance.

I'm sure each runner uses his own techniques of visualization, and maybe many don't use it at all; I will never presume to say that's what all runners should do. I do know that visualizing in the way I do helps give me a more positive outlook on the race before race day and during the race itself. Then when the race begins I can relax and run and just allow things to happen.

Before and during my 100 mile journey, I approach the awesome distance in a way mentally that will ease the pain, the discouragement, and the hopelessness. What I don't do is think of the entire 100 miles. I realize that in the back of my mind that half of us or more may fail, but that thought I block out completely. It does sound like a war where I know there will be casualties, but in my mind I think positive, that it will not happen to me because I will control and monitor my body throughout.

I have zeroed my thoughts into the fact that I will be out here for a long time, and I accept the fact. I am a machine that is fueled up for the next segment, and I know that I will be refueled when I get to the next pit stop. I can handle the shorter distances; I don't really want to think about what may be down the road. At times I really don't know my exact total distance when I reach an aid station, and if I do, it really doesn't sink in. 55 miles at Michigan Bluff has no meaning to me; all I know is that it's over six miles until Foresthill. I can't let myself day dream and envision crossing the finish line. That will come with time.

My guiding force as a distance runner is my patience. Through my long distances, I have become a more patient animal in regular life. I am not so quick to become irritated at delays that are unnecessary. I plod forward one step at a time, one mile at a time, one aid station at a time. Impatience means hurrying when it will cost me in the longer time of one day to reach my goal. I am the tortoise; I may be slow, but I will reach my destination; I just slide along, never going too fast but never stopping. When the race is over I will be there, while the faster hares may be suffering on the sidelines short of the finish line.

Failure does not exist, because to accept it is to invite it to happen, but in the back of my mind I know it is possible. I know I am physically prepared and mentally zeroed in. My goal is not to make it in 24 hours, but to do the best I can possibly do. I will stay on the 24 hour deadline and try to build up a small cushion; not a large cushion, because I will then become the hare. I will try to keep it as long as I can, and that is all I ask of myself. If it is close at the end, I will try for it. If it is not close, I can accept it. Whatever the results, I can accept them if I have given my best effort. However, it will be my very best effort because I will accept very few excuses for myself.

One day of solid running is a long time for anyone. To think of it in the sense of what I do during a normal day cracks a hole in my mind. I must smile a little when I think how ridiculous it can look to a normal non-running person. I can't take this whole event so seriously. 24 hours is really such a short time in the time of one's life. It is such a long time, yet it is so very short. It will be over before I can blink one eye. I blink that one eye or do I wink, telling time that he really is a joke? He really is only the movement of the earth, the rising and setting of the sun, the artificial clock that we humans have made for ourselves. Why 24 hours? Why not minutes of 40 seconds? How about hours of 75 minutes? It is all relative anyway. Time really doesn't exist for this race. It is the distance, the earth that I will cover with my feet, the trees, mountains, canyons, rivers, and nature's creatures that I will pass. I am really an explorer on an adventure. This is really no race for time; it is my body and mind meeting with the elements and trying to harmonize with them.

I am quiet in mind and soul when I run. It is what I like to do. For one day in my short lifetime I am experiencing life to the fullest, seeing everything within my soul. My body is ready; it is now the time to go, to do it, to move on and on and on and on....

One important quality of character a participant who hopes to complete the Western States must have is that of patience. In addition the same individual must be able to establish a tempo for the overall race. I use the word tempo rather than pace because pace implies to me setting the speed with which one runs according to the race course and maintaining that speed to finish the race. Tempo indicates the ability to change pace frequently according to the ups and downs and difficulty of the trail, yet establishing an overall philosophy of racing speed to finish the race.

Patience has more than the simple meaning of knowing one is going to be out there a long time and to not get in a hurry. Certainly this definition does apply and is an important one. Realizing that picking up the speed of the overall run to hurry to the finish will result in a non-finishing effort is certainly a key factor in one's success in the race. Being able to apply this patience in its many-headed ramifications during the run itself is the most important factor. Let me show what I mean.

Way before the race begins I run all of the course during several practice sessions. During a particular session I study the ups and downs, get to know the general footing of different sections of the trail, and evaluate how fast I can go on these sections during race day. I consider also how fatigued I will be at a certain point and whether or not I will be running at night or maybe during the hottest part of the day. I make a conservative estimate of how long it will take me to complete a certain section on race day, and I set up an overall time frame of the course based upon 23 and a half hours, allowing a 30 minute cushion. During the training sessions, I am in no particular hurry. My mind is alert to the trail; I try to grasp everything about the course and store these elements in my mind for later use during the race.

Then during the race when I must take an hour to walk three miles or more up a steep mountainside, I know I have planned for it and can or have made up that lost time on another part of the course. I don't panic

169

and try to run part of the hill to make up the lost time. That running will only unnecessarily wear me out physically, which will catch up to me later in the race.

Basically then I have the patience to know when I can go slowly, and even recover, and when I should pick up the speed, as on the downhill sections. My patience is like a clock that knows there are places on the course that are fast sections and places that are slow sections, and to accept these sections for what they really are. In the long term, if I show patience and run each section accordingly, the time will balance out at the finish line.

All this is difficult to do without running the course in practice and knowing it before the race begins. It is even more difficult for the first time entrant who badly wants his 24 hour buckle and for just an instant loses his patience and deviates from his game plan and attacks a slow section of the trail foolishly.

As I run the race I see only the next section ahead of me, often in terms of the time only, perhaps of both time and distance. I don't look past the next checkpoint; I zero in on completing the short distance of three, five, or maybe ten miles in a certain time based upon the uphills and downhills. I know ahead of time that I will run a certain downhill section fairly hard because I know when I get to the bottom I will recover by walking up the hill.

Let me give a few examples during the first half of the race. I know I don't need to hurry coming out of Duncan Canyon to Robinson Flat at 30 miles. I've already made up time just before that point. Besides, from Robinson Flat to Last Chance at 43 miles and even to the bottom of the canyon three miles later, I will have a fast 16 mile section of many downhills and levels, much of it on good dirt and gravel roads. There is one short uphill section during that entire part of the run. I will be able to travel fast, and being rested at 30 miles will help me. Then when I get to those two steep consecutive canyon climbs before Michigan Bluff at 55 miles in the heat of the day, I now can walk them, not worrying because I have built up my cushion during the previous fast section.

Patience means staying on this game plan throughout the entire race, avoiding the pitfalls of getting overexcited about losing time and trying to push it. I use my patience and knowledge of the trail as my ally, knowing that if I'm physically prepared for the race, I can get to the finish line.

A footbridge looms up at the bottom of a canyon.

Tied in with patience is the tempo I previously mentioned. I believe that in a race of this nature the runner doesn't set the tempo of his run; the trail dictates the tempo to the runner. The runner must know his or her own ability to cope with the physical stress of the run and thus adjust the individual tempo to the demands of a particular section of the trail.

My tempo changes to the course so it will always be just off the red line of running too hard. The race is too long and rigorous to be tired at 30 miles. If I feel that muscle or body fatigue is taking over half way through the race and the trail goes uphill, I have probably crossed that red line and must slow down no matter what the temporary cost in time may be. Once I have established a slow enough tempo to recover, even if it is a slow walk for 20 minutes, I can overcome my fatigue and pick up the tempo so it is just below the red line again.

How do I do this, and how do I know when and what kind of adjustments to make? Throughout the race I listen to my body very carefully for certain signs of weakening. I know myself thoroughly; I have trained for months and know what I am capable of. If a certain subtle point of fatigue is reached, I know from my miles of training that I must back off. If I back off, and I feel strength in my legs, experience tells me I can pick up the pace and I will feel all right. In the long haul, it is not important what other people tell me to do, but what I know I can do comfortably at that point to finish the 100 miles.

The whole idea of tempo is familiar to even the 10K racer, only the tempo or pace is much faster because the distance is so much shorter and the demands on the body so much less. The adjustments are easier to make because the runner can survive the last mile or so. During the long ultrarun survival of the last mile depends entirely on the tempo set early on. Of course, at a certain point in the race, like the last mile of a 10K, the runner is just trying to survive. In the 100 miler it might be the last ten miles or even 20 miles. If the correct tempo has been used early and throughout most of the race, the runner should be almost spent by the time the finish line is reached.

I finish this race partly because my tempo remains consistent throughout and I never try to push any part of it I know I shouldn't. When I have a period when I do feel strong, I do push it right to the edge of the red line. Fortunately I have some luck and my good periods are longer than my low periods. That is because of my conditioning. I make adjustments as I go, and I stay patient enough not to stray too far away from my game plan. I am fortunate that nothing major in my body malfunctions, and the final result is that I arrive at the finish line in the expected time.

There is no guarantee that everything will go well the next time I run the race. I can only prepare myself physically and mentally and try to do the best I can. If circumstances dictate that I fail in my quest, I know there will always be another day and another attempt.

Out on the trail only I know the pain and suffering that is happening to my body and mind. The trees and the trail don't care to hear my complaints. I run and walk, often pushing through the pain in my thighs, many times talking to myself to get my body to continue on through the discomfort. If anyone sees me now, I must look like a wreck of some kind.

I can't look this way when I reach my crew and the medical personnel. The medical people might not let me continue, although my crew will tell me I look great even though they know I am a destroyed wreck of a human body. It is time to put on my mask, my mask of looking and sounding like I'm just out for an easy, short stroll in the woods. I cannot reveal in any way how I really feel, not in any tone of voice, altered state of running, or expression on my face.

I pick up the pace a bit as I enter the aid station. I acknowledge the comments of the spectators and aid people who encourage me with a wave of a hand and a retort of some kind if appropriate, hopefully something a little bit humorous. They may laugh back, probably to humor me if it really isn't a funny comment. An aid person takes my pack, and I step lively and quickly on the scale, giving those checking me my starting weight in a sentence before they even ask for it. When my weight is good, I quip something to the fact that it better be because I've been drinking like a fish and feel as strong as a horse. All my positive comments and looks will probably get me through, although I may be still suffering underneath the screen I am hiding behind.

My crew is very considerate of my every need; I smile back even though my heart isn't smiling. I joke even though nothing is funny. I try to say something very lucid and intelligent even though I feel like my brain is numb. I use all the acting ability I never had in the first place, and I think I'm doing a great job. Time is going by too fast at this rest stop, but I make believe that it is really dragging. I tell my crew members that I feel quite good at this point and am anxious to start up again, when my legs are actually laughing at me sarcastically while I talk.

I sometimes don't really know whether these are my words coming from my lips. There must be a recording in my voice box, certainly not in my brain, which cannot believe all the strange words I am echoing. I am giving out specific instructions to my crew, not really knowing what I want. I try to answer their million questions about my well-being and what I need. I know what I really want, a chance to sit and languish, to not get up again and continue on. I know that won't go over too well, so dutifully I cheerfully stand and begin my trek again.

My mask has done a great job. They really believe that I feel fine. I stand up steadily and put my pack back on without fumbling with the belt. My legs still feel wobbly, but I start to walk and they begin to cheer. I make some positive parting comments that tell them that I will see them again at the next rendezvous point. They really think I am ready to charge to the next station. How easy it is to fool those who aren't running this deadly course of torture. They really believe I am feeling no pain and will finish the course with flying colors. The only color I am flying is red, the red pain digging deep into my legs and body, crying to stop but not with enough conviction to stop my madman's brain from pushing on.

I take off out of the aid station and people and voices begin to fade into the background. I'm back on my own again, where I can take my mask off again and quit playing the "feeling good" game. I reach up and peel off my smile and my mask and get back to business. Strange, but my mask refuses to come off no matter how hard I pull. The smile remains. An amazing transformation has taken hold before all these people and myself. I believe that I really do feel good, my legs are no longer sore, and that I can step out lively. Let the run continue.

Truly then, the race is more than the physical strength to push to the finish line. It becomes a combination of the physical with that element that all human beings possess, an intelligent mind. With that mind enters the soul and the combination is that what we call determination or heart. The Western States cannot be mastered until the contests of the mind have been won.

As I look down at the softly flowing river near where I grew up some 20 years after the race, I realize that I have always played these mind games to get me through difficult situations, whether it be physical, intellectual, or emotional. Life situations of difficulties have come up numerous times since the original race, yet I can use the same patience and positive attitude to get through these same difficulties.

For sure it isn't always easy, and there is still an emotional strain on my psyche whenever I have encountered these situations. But by relaxing for a moment and thinking through all the possible choices of actions and consequences I realize that I can only do the best I can at the moment and let the situation solve itself. All I need to do is recall the running of this race and I realize that things will work out somehow. Certainly even if they don't work out perfectly, it's not the end of the world.

One thing you find out when you get older is that you can actually calculate actions that appear to be perhaps off the edge of behavior. People often believe you are actually this way in all aspects in life, but in reality a lot of it is acting and this acting is used to perhaps achieve some immediate purpose. You play these mind games with the people you deal with to accomplish certain goals because you know it is necessary, yet all the while it is not who you really are. The mind games of life certainly make life in general more interesting.

The same mind games on the trail also make life on the trail more interesting. They also provide that necessary edge to help you to reach the finish line. In life these same games can also help you to reach the end of life's trails. They work only if you truly know your own inherent self, the real you and what you want out of life and living.

CHAPTER 20
PERSONAL CONSIDERATIONS

Running ultra long distances is obviously not for everyone. To urge every competitive runner to attempt the Western States is a fallacy. Even those runners who run fast times in the 10K, half marathon, and marathon may not be suited for an ultrarun. One of the reasons I race them is because I feel I have certain natural endurance abilities which allow me to complete the runs. I have discovered these abilities over many years of running and have worked very hard to enhance them, to bring them out to their full potential.

Many of these endurance qualities I knew I had to some degree based upon other experiences in the past. I discovered even other traits as I continued to build on my personal training and racing experiences. One reason I ran the Western States is that I felt I had an opportunity to bring out these abilities. Certainly I'm not even close to being any type of major, top class endurance athlete, but I have found some things I can do well in relation to other sporting activities, and running super-long distances seems to be one of those assets.

First of all, I was born on a hill and grew up as a child in the mountains. Everywhere I walked, played, and ran was up and down. In addition, the woods, the old, beat up dirt roads, winding trails, and gentle streams were part of my childhood playground. Even though as an adult I live in a flat, concrete infested world, I always yearn to return to the natural ways of my youth. I am totally at home in the mountains, in the beckoning wilderness trails of my childhood. I don't travel them to view the scenery; the immediate trails and mountains themselves are my scenery. I only need to glance around my present area. I am comfortable in the environment of the Western States trail because it is so much like what I grew up in as a young child.

I don't need a lot of practice to become accustomed to the roughness of the trail because I have always known such trails. I need only to adjust my legs to the uphills and downhills; it is not something new to me. I have been going up and down since I was old enough to take my first steps. I don't remember just how old I was when I first discovered that there were flat spots in the world. Everything I knew early in my life was tilted.

Crossing a stream, a puddle, or a wide river is almost as natural to me as walking. In training runs with friends in the woods, I often quickly rock hop a stream and start again while my faster friends are still carefully and methodically considering what rock to step on next. I have spent many long hours fly fishing small to large streams, wading up to my thighs or higher, negotiating rocks, rapids, and swift, deep pools. I am totally comfortable around flowing water. I have tamed it for most of my life. I can truly say that the River Crossing was one of the most exciting highlights of my run.

I have never been very fast as an athlete but certainly not the slowest either. Often somewhat overweight, speed has never been my best asset, although I can occasionally do fairly well at shorter distances. I enjoy running the faster races like a 10K, but it is hard work for me. I am sometimes even competitive in my age group. However, there are just too many rabbits out there for me to do well. Doing the short races week after week can often become boring and even meaningless. My times are usually close to the same every time out, and I know I will always finish the race somehow. The challenge for speed is present, but I don't possess much of it, so the competitive feeling pales after awhile.

However, I have always done well athletically in events involving endurance, often during great periods of time. I must have an inherited trait of endurance somewhere in my background. I have snow skied all my life and can go all day without much of a break. Before I began running, for several summers I would backpack solo in the high Sierras, often as much as eight to ten days at one stretch, covering 10 to 20 miles a day, camping and fishing along the way, with a fully loaded pack on my back. I never did any training for these hikes. I simply went out and did them. Friends and I used to always go on day long fishing excursions, often into and out of canyons, sometimes covering 10 miles or more in the course of a day, plus a day of fishing. All of this hiking built up the power in my legs even when I weighed 25 to 30 pounds more than I do as a runner. I look back and realize that all this hiking was very natural to me, an activity where I continued to endure.

I never participated in endurance events as a youth, but I always remember in the military service how I would finish near the front in the two mile run in combat boots. I also learned cross country skiing and took to it easily. I competed as a lark in one race in the service and placed very high in the race. In college I would enter the intramural distance events and do decently well. I could go out and play tennis for long periods of time without wilting. All of this was an extension of my natural ability to endure.

I'm not sure whether the ability to recover quickly from a long endurance event is an ability or just determination, but I always remember having this trait. I might take a long, difficult 15 mile hike one day, ending up totally exhausted, and then get up the next morning ready to go again. When I am training well, I have no problem doing double workouts or back to back long runs in two days, as long as I don't have to worry about going out fast. I can feel very tired one moment, but give me a short break and I can be up and moving strongly again very shortly.

Some people are not suited for super endurance events because of their obsession with speed. They always train at a fast pace and can never do long runs very well because they always go too fast. Their object is always to run fast and get to their destinations quickly. To these runners, everything is run with a clock. There is nothing wrong with this type of running, but an ultrarun would be difficult for this competitor to even be able to finish because of the lack of sense of pace for the distance and certainly because of the missing element of patience to run slowly for a long period of time.

I do occasionally run and time myself but more important for me is the act of running continuously for a long period of time. Patience to keep moving is an asset I have; I feel no urge to hurry to beat the clock every time I go out to train. I don't set deadlines or always plan how many miles I will complete at a certain speed before I even take my first steps on a training outing. I have the super non-hurried attitude to finish a long race. I believe this all reflects my growing up attitude of not being in a hurry on the trails. An occasional 10K type of race lets me test myself against the clock, and that challenge is usually enough to last me for quite awhile. Since I don't have blazing speed I find that often during high, slow mileage training periods, I will record very fast times in shorter races simply on leg strength alone.

Although I don't possess great speed, some of my running friends are astounded that I can keep going for so long a time without stopping. Probably my biggest physical and mental ability is to keep on moving hour after hour. I often have trouble in training runs with friends on good surfaces, hills or not, because I can't relate my training sequence of run and recover to theirs of running all out most of the time. I don't give up if I feel badly for awhile; I just back off for a few moments and then resume my previous speed. I think this ability to literally recover on the run is maybe the strongest aspect of my overall endurance running.

All this discussion is to show one reason why I run ultras. The esoteric reasons of running come under a different subject. They are probably even more important in the overall scheme of why all of us run. What I hope here is to point out that I run long races because I have a reasonably natural ability to do fairly well in them. I know the strengths of my body and these strengths are suited for long races. My mental temperament is just right for these races. The ultra is a type of race that so few people can do well, and I find I am one of those select few. Most of us like to pursue further what we have the ability to do well; I am no exception to that rule.

After completing successfully a race like the Western States, it is almost frightening to run a short race, because suddenly some of my friends may consider me somewhat better than what I really am. In the short race I am back to earth, in the middle to front fourth of the pack, just another runner. My co-called super powers can't be use here, and my good running friends are back ahead of me again. Yet, I need to run these races if for any other reason to bring myself back to reality. Although no one can ever take that buckle away from me, I need to remember my roots and that there are never ending tests that await for me around each corner. I must always continue to test my ability in all types of races at all kinds of different distances.

One of the main reasons for success in this race is pure luck. I feel very lucky that one of any number of countless mishaps that could have befallen me did not occur. Anywhere out there on the trail, a sudden and unsuspecting demon can step out and knock me physically or mentally off the trail before my task is accomplished.

I am a prepared animal physically to run this race, so why do I need luck? The fascination, the almost frightening aspect of a course like this, is its unpredictability. I can be totally fit and mentally prepared to do well, but the course is so demanding, so changing, and so very, very long that the unexpected can happen to even the best runners. Luck is a major part of success and failure, but some of this luck can be controlled, can be manipulated by the prepared runner. However, some of it is out of the runner's conscious efforts to control. It is that type of luck, good or bad, that can make or break a runner's race. How lucky was I to be able to finish the race?

The author, right, poses after the American River 50 with two outstanding ultrarunners and friends, David Calderon and Jeff Pierce.

First, I don't become injured in a fall. The one fall I take is within the first 30 miles and it comes on a smooth, debris covered section of gradual, downhill trail. I am running easily and quickly, and temporarily take my focus off the trail itself. My mind drifts away slightly and I stop picking up my feet like I should, instead shuffling lazily across the dirt carpet. Small rocks jut out of the narrow trail, and I trip over one. I sprawl forward and sideways and catch myself with my hands on the soft surface.

The fall wakes me up and I never face another fall again, even over the roughest, rockiest terrain, the steep uphills and downhills. Often I tell myself out loud to slow down and don't do anything foolish, to pick up my feet carefully and watch each individual foot plant. Is it luck that I never fall and injure myself? Even the most careful runner can make a sudden error over 100 miles and lose it all. I am as careful as I possibly can be, but, yes, I have a lot of luck too.

I run and walk for 100 miles, nearly 24 hours, eating and drinking, and I have virtually no major stomach problems. I vomit twice during the race, but each time the sickness comes quickly and suddenly, I don't lose much from my stomach, and I feel much better after each occurrence. During a couple of marathons, one 50 miler, and several long training runs, I have experienced virtually no stomach problems at all despite all the trauma my system encounters. My stomach almost seems to shift into a neutral gear and seems determined not to be a factor at all in the race. Is this luck? I feel like it probably is luck. At least I didn't encounter the added burden of having to handle such problems.

Nowhere do my legs finally give out because of pain and fatigue. At times they become tired, sore, and very heavy, but short rests and walks seem to always revive them again and again. The vicious downhills do not wreck my quads or my knees. I survive it all, the rough trails, the endless miles, the long hours, without my legs giving out. Is that luck? Maybe, but I like to believe my training and my peaking at the right time has some major influence on my success.

Not once during the race do I ever pull a muscle, twist an ankle, wrench a knee, or find some slow, spreading pain creeping throughout some part of my body which might slow me down. One awkward step on a rock or twist in a hole and it can be all over for me. Those slow pains of hidden injury can come quickly, hideously, and unsuspecting upon the runner intent on placing one foot in front of the other. Am I lucky here? I know I am in great shape, but even the best conditioned athletes encounter these kinds of injuries, so I guess I have some luck on my side.

Blisters! The race director says he would like to meet any runner who does the entire race without getting a blister. Well, such a beast exists because I did not get one blister. Sure, I have some bruises on my ankles, and my feet are sore in a couple of specific places, but I have no blisters at all. I always notice that I rarely get blisters in marathons or 50 milers so I hope it holds over to a 100 miler and fortunately it does. Is this being lucky? Well, I change shoes two times and my socks about six times. My shoes fit me well for the trails and I run with a fairly normal stride. Despite this I am probably still lucky that blisters didn't slow me down.

Never during the race do I encounter fatigue or sleepiness. At 3 a.m. I still feel alert and my mind is focused. I remember clearly almost every part of the race. I don't need coffee, No Doz, or any other stimulant. I probably get no more than four hours of sleep the night before the race, so I should by all rights get sleepy and tired by remaining up all the next night. However, my intense concentration to finish under 24 hours keeps my spirits up and mentally I don't become discouraged. I have a goal to accomplish and I am having success. Is it lucky that I don't suddenly crash physically with massive fatigue and sleepiness? Maybe it is luck, but I hope to think a major part of it is that I have mentally and physically prepared myself for a goal, and that my intense concentration keeps me alert and awake throughout the race.

Yes, luck is a major factor in completing the race. Many of the top runners never reach the finish line, and many who are normally much faster than I am, finish hours behind me. The runner prepares himself the best he can, toes the starting line on race day, and hopes nothing drastic will go wrong. There is an underlying fear here not present in shorter races, because almost everyone finishes these. In this race half the runners may have to drop out, and each runner knows he might be one of them and that there is nothing that can be done about it. Everyone watching will see such a failure.

I am prepared for my race in every way, but I accept the good luck that is with me on that day during that race. Along with all the physical and mental preparation, pure and simple, it turns out to be my special day.

One of my non-running friends sees me several days after the race is over and asks me if I am through with such foolishness now that I have done the race. My immediate reaction is that I have never considered it foolish in the first place; in fact, I have always considered it another normal challenge that so many of us pass up in this very short life we live, a life that can often keep us in little shells, never to experience some of the very unique opportunities that await us.

I enjoy most of the non-running activities that I am involved in, but I consider my running as something special and very high on my list of life's priorities. I don't have to justify to anyone who doesn't understand why I run this race why I am doing it. Besides they usually don't understand. No, I don't consider running the Western States foolishness; the learning experience has been very valuable to all the other activities in my life.

I think the most important thing I learn is the development of a strong feeling of patience when frustration is about to set in. I have always had a contradictory trait, I feel, in that I will jump to anger at times very quickly, yet I will persevere on something that I know will take time. From this race, even when I do become angry, it recedes very quickly and I am able to back off more quickly. My perseverance or patience to accomplish something is even stronger, and I don't let some of the little obstacles get me down. I know that time will solve the problem.

In conjunction I believe I don't take so many of the little irritating things in life as seriously as I used to. Someone does something that irritates me, or a friend gets angry with me, and I pass it off and forget about it because I know that it is a temporary problem that the other person has. Getting through this race in one piece and with a fair amount of success has taught me that these upsetting happenings really aren't that important. The problem will again pass with time, the person usually doesn't mean it, and it doesn't do any good to get upset anyway. The only serious things in this world are people who are starving and homeless, and people who lack love and self-esteem.

This race is not foolishness because I would be a fool if I didn't take advantage of the natural talents God has given me. I don't want to end up a retired old man looking back on all the things I should have done. I want to be able to say that I tried them. I believe the problem with most people is that they stay locked up in the same old rut year after year, never venturing out to test themselves. My favorite saying still is, "Only those who risk going too far can possibly find out how far one can go." I want to find out how far I can go, and I am finding out that it is a lot further than I ever vaguely imagined. I'm sure I haven't found the limit yet. We human beings are really remarkable creatures.

As an educator I preach motivation and trying to do one's best. I advocate hard work to accomplish those things that are worthwhile in life. How can I preach this doctrine if I don't practice it myself? In my ultrarunning I must sacrifice time and train way beyond what the normal body would expect. I believe I am practicing far beyond anything my students will have to do. When I talk about these attributes to my students, my example demonstrates to them that I really believe in what I say and that I am an excellent model of what I preach.

My race of 100 miles is not foolish. The word comes from fool, which according to the dictionary is a person lacking in judgment or prudence, or a harmlessly deranged person or one lacking in common powers of understanding. It is true that some of my non-running friends really believe

I lack judgment, but judgment is a decision or conclusion based upon all the facts at hand, or doing something based upon one's preparedness and understanding of the task and its consequences. Before running this 100 mile run I certainly prepare myself both physically and mentally, and I carefully weigh all the facts of preparedness and understand just what I am getting into. My decision to run, some might say, is based on pure courage. In fact, it is based on cold, calculated evaluation of the facts of my being able to run the race.

So many of us live really boring lives. We may think we are extremely happy, and maybe we are to some degree. To many people the good life is being retired, sitting around the pool, relaxing in front of the television set or with a good book, or going on a cruise doing the same things. I admire these people if they really believe the good life is theirs.

I can't sit back and let the world come to me, although out of necessity there are times when I will temporarily accept this kind of living as a recovery period before I do something else. There comes a time though when I must leave the comfortable nest to physically and mentally challenge my environment, to seek the opportunities to do something exciting and new, something fresh to dare my courage and soul, to reaffirm the inside of my heart which tells me I'm a worthwhile person with some purpose for being on this earth, a seemingly insignificant ant in a sea of millions.

Whatever I do, it must involve some kind of supreme effort or the world will become boring for me and will be without purpose. I happen to have found this challenge in my running life. No, my running this race is not foolishness, yes, I would do this race again, and yes, someday I may look for even a bigger challenge to see if I can really ever find out how far I can go.

I continued with my running after the Western States. The race spurred me on to do many more marathons and ultras. Gradually my times began to slow until it was a very fast downhill slide. I ran a second Western States three years after the first one with a much slower time of 26:48. In many ways it was just as satisfying as the first one, because this time I managed to survive on less training. I proved one more time that finishing the race was more important than time.

As aging began to affect my legs and body, I did fewer and fewer of the long runs. The ultras become slow 50 kilometer trail runs. The times in the marathons began to approach and then go past four hours. The body was showing the effects of all the years of pounding and the natural wearing out that occurs when we get older, a condition that none of us can avoid forever. My last ultra race was a 50 kilometer run in 1997. My final marathon was a very slow 4:42 run in 2001. Before it was all over I had completed 35 marathons and 39 ultramarathons. During the past few years I have been able to do only an occasional recreation run no longer than a 5K or 10K.

My mind and spirit still would like to run like I used to, but the body now says no to the demand. I have accepted that answer and continue to train at a much slower pace and walk when necessary. I feel badly sometimes when I can't really cut it loose like the old days and run all out for a big race. Yet, I realize that I had the opportunity to experience something few others will ever attempt. It is nice to know when the challenge was there in front of me, I was able to meet it head on and become successful beyond my wildest dreams.

My journeys across these race courses brought to me some wild and crazy landscapes and scenery, gave me an opportunity to go places that I wouldn't have seen otherwise. Whether it was on urban courses or remote wilderness trails, the journey allowed me to see places that I wouldn't have ordinarily experienced. Whether it was running down an echo-filled almost vacant Market Street in San Francisco or shuffling cautiously along a narrow trail perched a thousand feet directly above a roaring stream, my consciousness is forever full of all that the world has to offer.

If I can no longer run these long distances physically, I can still run them in my mind, reliving every step along the way. Now I take my physical paths elsewhere, whether it be hiking on those same trails I once ran or racing down a black diamond ski run on the back side of Northstar at Lake Tahoe. My running journey appears almost over, but my life's journey is still a long way from the finish line.

CHAPTER 21
TRAINING LOG

I officially begin my training schedule for the Western States several weeks before I know I have been accepted. Prior to beginning my specified training, I have been running about 40 miles per week during the past couple of months. I usually allow the fall season as a time for recovery and thus cut back on my mileage during that time. I hope to get an early start on my base mileage for the race, and even if I'm not accepted, this mileage will serve me well for other marathons and 50 mile races I plan to do during the spring. The schedule runs 30 weeks leading up to race day and is not completely or formally planned ahead of time. I end up by averaging 80 miles per week for the 29 weeks leading up to the race, with a low of 35 miles and a high of 108 miles. My biggest month is May when I log 400 miles.

I keep a daily log on all my runs, with some pertinent information on each run such as pace, terrain, and how I feel. In addition to my running I do at least 100 pushups and 200 situps daily to strengthen other parts of my body. I often plan my runs according to how much time I have available; my running schedule must fit around my working and social schedule. My main goal early on is to build up a good high mileage base, and to add to that later the necessary tuning on the hills and trails. I plan several key long races to use as preparation for the Western States; a couple of them are cancelled and I have to make a couple of changes in my plans. My goal is to run at a pace in other races where I can go out comfortably the next day and do five or six miles without much after effect. That plan holds true to form in almost all my races.

My training weeks begin on Saturday and end on Friday. Here then are the highlights of each week of my preparation. I will only discuss my longer runs or ones of significance.

WEEK 1: November 30 to December 6: I run an easy 17 miles on Saturday and 13 miles on Sunday for a total of 30 weekend miles. Three of those miles on Sunday are run at a 6:32 pace. On Tuesday I do 11 miles, including running the steps for a couple of miles at the local football stadium. I return with 13.5 miles on Wednesday and 10 on Thursday. With my other days of shorter mileage I total 80.5 miles for the week.

WEEK 2: December 7 to December 13: My big workout is 20.5 miles on Sunday, divided into two separate sessions. I do 8 miles in the morning, including a 10K race at 39:59. I then add 12.5 miles in the evening using my favorite run/walk technique. I usually run for 17 minutes and walk for 3 minutes or use any other combination that gives 8 to 12 minutes of brisk recovery walking per hour. After an easy Monday, I rattle off 14 miles in two workouts on Tuesday, including 3.5 miles at a 7 minute pace. This pace may not seem very fast but is a definite pickup from my long, slow mileage. I tack on 10.5 miles on Wednesday and 13.5 on Thursday, giving me three good workouts in a row. My total for the week including a couple of shorter workouts comes out to 80.5 miles.

WEEK 3: December 14 to December 20: My big run is on Sunday with 24 miles which covers two workouts. In the morning I run a Rocky II. Our club's Rocky Hill workout is an 8.5 mile loop which includes two long steep hills, both up and down. A Rocky II is two loops of this workout. I add the rest of the miles in the evening on the flat. I follow that workout with four straight days of over 10 miles each day, each workout done on the flat. The miles for the days are 11, 11.5, 14.5, and 10. My second day I do some informal speed play of 100 to 300 yards, and on my third day of the four, I do track intervals, including 2X330, 2X440, 4X220, and 6X110 yards. My total for the week is 81 miles.

WEEK 4: December 21 to December 27: On Saturday I do 12.5 easy miles at a 17/3 run/walk regiment. I follow this up with 10 miles on Sunday at an easy pace. On Monday I run 11.5 miles on all hills, including 4 over dirt and rutted roads with snow and ice. Wednesday I run 14.5 miles on all very steep hills with snow and mud at a slow ultra pace of 11:43 per mile, concentrating mainly on keeping my footing. On Friday I add 16 miles on hills, including 7.5 on trails with some snow at a 10:48 pace. My total for the week is 74 miles.

WEEK 5: December 28 to January 3: On Sunday I run 11.5 miles, 4 of them on flat terrain and 7.5 on steep, paved hills. Monday I take on a 30 mile run at an overall 10:30 pace on both flat and hilly terrain. I follow these workouts with four straight days of over 10 miles per day, which includes workouts of 10.5, 14, 17,and 13 miles. Six miles of the 17 mile workout are done on hills. My total for the week is exactly 100 miles, the first time I have ever reached this total in all my running career.

WEEK 6: January 4 to January 10: My big workout is 30.5 miles on Sunday with 25 of those miles in the morning and 5.5 in the evening. I do 12 miles on Monday which includes the following intervals: 12X110 and 8X220. I add 15 more miles on Wednesday, which includes several sub-8 minute miles and 2 miles at a 7:20 pace. I follow that up with another 15 miles on Thursday in 2 hours and 40 minutes at a slow 10:40 ultra pace. My total for the week is 93 miles.

WEEK 7: January 11 to January 17: I run a total of 20.5 miles on Saturday, including 18 at once at a very hard 6:46 pace, just under 2 hours and 2 minutes. I do 17 miles the next day in two workouts. Monday I run 11.5 miles, Tuesday I add 11 miles, Wednesday I increase to 13 miles, and on Thursday I run 12 miles, some at a sub-7:30 pace. My complete weekly total comes out to 90 miles. So far I haven't done any exceptionally long runs, but have tried to string five or six days in a row of double figure mileage workouts. I can feel the strength in my legs gradually building up with these constant repetitions of long workouts. My recovery from day to day is also improving dramatically.

WEEK 8: January 18 to January 24: My big workout comes on Sunday with 24.5 miles, including a 10K in the morning at a big PR of 37:26. I add a 16.5 mile workout in the hills in the afternoon at a 10 minute pace. My huge endurance base pays off in the 10K as I run it simply on leg strength alone and maintain a strong, even pace throughout the race. After an easy Monday, I run 15 miles on Tuesday, 10 of them between a 7 and 7:30 pace. I do slow workouts the next two days of 13.5 and 13 miles. Each day I do a couple of miles of vigorous walking in the evening. My total mileage for the week comes to 86.5.

WEEK 9: January 25 to January 31: This is an easy week because I have a marathon coming up the next Saturday. I do 11 miles on Saturday and 22.5 miles on Sunday which includes a Rocky II of 17 miles on the hills. I do 11.5 more on Monday and then easier workouts between 2 and 9 per day the rest of the week. My total for the week is 68 miles. After 9 weeks of winter base training I have averaged nearly 84 miles per week and now am ready to start adding marathons and 50 mile races to my training schedule, and even cutting back my mileage on some weeks.

Now comes the time to prepare myself for the rest of the race itself in phase two of my training by racing distances from a marathon on up to a 12 hour run.

WEEK 10: February 1 to February 7: On Saturday I run the Bakersfield Marathon, a basic flat course in 3:36. I finish strong even though I do feel somewhat tired at the end of the race. On Sunday I come right back with a 13.5 mile workout, including 10 miles at Rocky Hill, 8 of those vigorous hill miles. Then suddenly comes one of my biggest fears, a physical setback that interrupts my training. I develop a virus and become ill. My running is limited to just a total of about 7 miles for the remainder of the week. My weekly total is just 47 miles.

WEEK 11: February 8 to February 15: This is my most disastrous mileage week of my entire training cycle. Because of my illness I get in only 35 miles, a good portion walking, and over half comes during the last two days. I have a big decision to make: whether to run the Jedediah Smith 50 in Sacramento on the following Sunday. I debate back and forth, unable to make up my mind whether to race. Finally I test myself two days before the race and decide to run it to get my qualifying time of under 10 hours. I do feel much better by now.

WEEK 12: February 16 to February 21: I'm back in form again. I run the 50 mile race in a blinding rain and wind storm and run a 8:38 to qualify in a very conservative effort. It becomes a good test of my overall training level and the fact that I have recovered from my illness. I feel fine physically during the entire race and experience only a little bit of soreness after the race. I come back with runs of 7, 10.5, and 8 miles on Tuesday through Thursday, finishing the week with 84 miles. I am back on schedule.

WEEK 13: February 22 to February 28: My big workout is on Saturday when I do almost 32 miles, 26 coming at Rocky Hill in the morning at a slow, steady pace, and the rest coming in an evening run. On Wednesday I run 18 miles, 6 in the morning and 12 in the evening, including some miles where I pick up the pace to a 7:30. I add 11 miles on Friday, including numerous speed bursts of 100 to 500 yards. With the shorter runs on the other days, I run a total of 87 miles for the week.

WEEK 14: March 1 to March 7: After an easy Saturday workout, I run 27 miles in the morning on Sunday with a 17 minute run, 3 minute walk sequence at an overall pace of just under 11 minutes per mile. On Monday I run 10 miles, including speed work of 5X one third miles and 5X150 yard speed bursts. Wednesday I run 11.5 miles with hard speed work of 12X220. I add 14.5 miles over the last two days. My total mileage for the week is 75.

WEEK 15: March 8 to March 14: I do a 25 mile workout on Saturday and 20 on Sunday in a run/walk sequence. I add 13.5 miles on Monday, this time picking up the pace with two medium hard miles and 7X180 yard bursts. After an easy Tuesday, I do 11.5 on Wednesday, including many slow miles along with frequent non-timed speed bursts between 100 and 400 yards. After an easy Thursday and Friday to rest for a marathon on Saturday, I total 81 miles for the week.

WEEK 16: March 15 to March 21: On Saturday I run the Porterville Marathon in a fine 3:14, a 7:26 pace. I recover quickly and the next day I do a 20 mile workout at a steady slow pace. I do fairly easy workouts the next three days, until Thursday when I run 11.5 miles, including four surges of one mile each at a 7:15 pace. My total mileage for the week is 83.

WEEK 17: March 22 to March 28: This is the highest mileage week of all my training, a total of 108 miles. The high total is because of a 12 hour track race on Sunday. Four of us start the run, two quitting after 31 miles. The other runner does 59 miles and I manage 64 miles and 3 laps before the 12 hour deadline. I feel fairly strong at the end of the run. After an easy day, I test my conditioning level with runs of 13, 14, and 10 miles on Tuesday, Wednesday , and Thursday. Most of the miles are done slowly, except the 10 miler, which is done entirely on the hills. I find my knee is a little sore, the old tendinitis coming back just slightly.

WEEK 18: March 29 to April 4: On Saturday I join a large group of other Western States entrants in an organized training run on the new 16 mile California Street Loop. My pacer Rob and I run it together and take it fairly hard. Our quads are sore for several days afterwards. The next day we run from the finish to No Hands Bridge and back. Later in the week on Wednesday, I run 10.5 miles, including 4.5 on Rocky Hill, and on Thursday I run 12 miles, including two, 3 mile stride outs at a 7 to 7:20 minute pace. My total for the week is 72 miles.

WEEK 19: April 5 to April 11: It is the week before my favorite 50 mile race, the American River 50. On Saturday I run 14 miles on Rocky Hill, and on Sunday I do 13.5 miles, including a 10K race in a time of 39:25, good time on no rest. After two days of easy mileage I do 10 miles on Wednesday with speed work that includes 8X110, 5X220, and 3X440. The rest of the week is easy in preparation for the race. Total miles for the week is an easy 53.

WEEK 20: April 12 to April 18: On Sunday I run the American River

50 in 8:52, about 30 minutes slower than my goal. The good feature is that I am strong at the finish and my conservative approach leads to a quick recovery. My only other hard workout is 12 miles the following Wednesday, with a little speed included in the run. For the week I total 82 miles.

WEEK 21: April 19 to April 25: It is now just ten weeks until the race, time to pick up the tempo even more than I have for the past several months, including more hills, more tough races, and a hard month of May training. On Saturday I run a very hilly 10K race in the morning in 42:18 and then drive to the mountains and run 13 miles of trail on snow and running water. I come back with 21 more miles on Sunday, all of it on flat terrain. The next four days I do workouts of 10, 8.5, 10, and 12 miles, the last workout including about 8 miles at a 7 to 8 minute per mile pace. My total miles for the week is 85.

WEEK 22: April 26 to May 2: I run one of my toughest back to back workouts on the weekend. I total 54 miles for the two days, 42 of them coming on hills. Saturday I run 30 miles, including 26 on a tough trail run up and back down the Kaweah River. On Sunday I run the tough Kaweah River 8 mile race in 56:53, add 8 miles right afterwards and do 7.5 miles in the evening. After two easy days, I run 13.5 miles on Wednesday on Rocky Hill and add 11 miles on Thursday. My total weekly mileage comes to 92.

WEEK 23: May 3 to May 9: Traveling on Saturday, I run the Wild, Wild West Cross Country Marathon in under 3:46, excellent in a very difficult race. I have short workouts on Monday and Tuesday, including some speed work on Tuesday. I do a split workout on Wednesday, totaling 15 miles, including some short, fast, intervals. My modest weekly total comes to 72 miles.

WEEK 24: May 10 to May 16: A vigorous trail workout including some very steep hills along with plenty of snow is in store on Saturday in Sequoia National Park. A group of us total about 32 miles in about 7.5 hours of moving. The next day I do 17.5 miles at an easy pace in 2 hours and 45 minutes. On Tuesday I total 16 miles in three separate workouts, including 9 miles at Rocky Hill on hills and dirt trails. I add a solid 12.5 miles on Thursday, pushing the pace and including 5X220 very fast stride outs. My total miles for the week come to 94.

WEEK 25: May 17 to May 23: I run back to back 20 mile efforts. On Saturday I run a 10K race in 41:27. In the afternoon I cover 14 miles in

3 hours and 40 minutes in extreme heat again in the afternoon. Tuesday I run 13.5 miles again in the heat. I do one stretch of 7 miles, beginning at a 10 minute pace and gradually increasing my pace until I am running the last couple under a 7 minute pace. On Thursday four of us go up to the mountains for a night run to check out the use of flashlights. We do 12 miles on a very steep, rough trail, 6 miles up and 6 miles back. Getting back late, I take Friday off from running. My total for the week is a high quality 78 miles.

WEEK 26: May 24 to May 30: I once again join other Western States runners on a training run from Robinson Flat to Michigan Bluff, one of the toughest sections of the course. The 26 miles take me about 6 hours, but I feel good at the end of the outing. The next day I take two practice runs, part of the California Street Loop and from the Highway 49 crossing to No Hands Bridge and back. The total mileage for the two days is 51. On Monday I do 13 miles on Rocky Hill in the extreme heat. I follow this run up with 10 and 12 miles the next two days. Taking Friday off before a 50 mile race, I still total another high quality 92 miles.

WEEK 27: May 31 to June 6: On Saturday my pacer Rob and I run the Nugget 50 Miler after driving for five hours the afternoon before to get there. We cruise this very difficult, mountain course in 10:17, a slow time only because I want something left for the big race in four weeks. I feel very comfortable at the end of the race. Rob and I get up on Sunday and enter a local 10K race. I run a 46:39 on a hilly course. I do 5 more miles that evening after arriving home. Tuesday I cover 11 miles in the heat with stride outs and fast walking. Wednesday I do 10 miles including speed work of 8X110, 4X440, 5X330, and 6X220. Thursday and Friday are easy days. My total mileage for the week is 93.

WEEK 28: June 7 to June 13: The hill training is now intensifying. I run with our training group 30 miles from Squaw Valley to Robinson Flat in 8 hours and 20 minutes over a lot of snow. I feel great at the end, hardly pressed at all. The next three days I do 11.5, 9, and 10 miles in 90 degree plus heat. I travel north to the Mt. Shasta area to spend a week on the trails. On Thursday I run 15 miles on the Pacific Crest Trail in 3 hours. On Friday I run 11 miles on the slopes of Mt. Shasta, through rough trails and lots of melting snow. I total 92 very tough miles for the week, and I feel almost ready.

WEEK 29: June 14 to June 20: I do five straight days of nothing but running the hills. Saturday I run 10 miles on a hilly road. Sunday I take on another 21 miler on the Pacific Crest Trail. After 5 and 8 miles the next two days, I do my final last long run Wednesday, June 18, 21 miles again on the Pacific Crest Trail. The scenery is magnificent and it is now time to gear down my training. Thursday and Friday are easy for a total of 70 miles.

WEEK 30: June 21 to June 27: I run 6.5 miles on Saturday and a solid one loop on Rocky Hill of 8.5 miles on Sunday. I run an easy 6 miles on Monday and 5.5 on Tuesday. Wednesday I travel to the race site. Thursday and Friday are days of rest. During the last 6 weeks the slight tendinitis in my left knee acts up only when I'm not running. It's sore a little the night before the race, but ice, a night's sleep, and I'm ready to take off on my adventure Saturday morning, June 28, 1986.

After the 1989 finish: Rob Stephenson, the author, crew chief Richard Rodriguez, Len Hansen, the author's sister Kathy Enea.

Whew - after all that I am amazed that I was able to complete the race. Still today I like to keep precise records of many of my daily routines, perhaps trying to learn something about myself. Relying on memory alone doesn't work for me. What I thought I accomplished and what the reality of the situation ended up being are usually different. I see clearly it is a part of human nature to distort our experiences as we get older, making the accomplishments more generous than what they really were, or weakening

194

the disasters in our lives, making them less serious than the reality. Maybe that is part of making our lives more liveable when we have to deal with past deeds.

Looking back from the chair I am now sitting in, I realize that I kept this running log while it was happening. It is not a figment of my imagining mind, trying to put a spin on just how good a shape I was in at the time of the race. At the time of the real race, I had doubts that I could finish it and even greater doubts that I could make it under 24 hours. Yet I was able to relax and go do the seemingly impossible for a runner of average running talents. At least today I perceive that as the real situation that occurred 20 years. Did I successfully reach the finish as part of an accident or a part of a great athletic upset. The upset is that unexpected victory that occurs when no one expects it. On a personal competitive level it is even more difficult to evaluate an upset, because the expectations are very personal. When I asked my running friends later how they thought I might do, most believed as I did that I was on the margin of breaking the 24 hour barrier.

Looking back on the training log, I see now that there was no reason to doubt that I would break 24 hours. One thing that stands out for sure was that I was totally prepared to the best of my ability to have a good day. I did everything possible under my control to make sure that I would make it to the finish line in a good time. Only circumstances out of the ordinary, which in this race happen all the time, could keep me from my appointment with the finishing banner before the sun came up that summer Sunday morning.

Seeing myself now 20 years later I am not amazed that I made it. I was completely prepared for anything the course threw at me and I was in the best physical condition of my life, a total endurance running machine. The race confirmed for me a valuable lesson that I had always tried to apply in every goal I was reaching for. It is a lesson that I have continued to reinforce for the past 20 years. The lesson is that to accomplish anything in life, one must be totally committed and prepared with every fiber of one's heart and soul.

I no longer keep detailed training logs. I do keep a brief log of my mileage, but that includes both walking and jogging and I don't break it down into separate categories. However, I try to prepare myself completely to meet any stones and logs that come along my life's trail and try to trip me up. The trail in many ways is steeper and more difficult than it used to be. The journey may be much slower and tedious, but my steps are always going forward, wary of the obstacles, prepared to meet and match myself against the seen and unseen demons that I may encounter along the way. One thing I know on my journey is that I will always be prepared to take the next step forward.

The training log of my life's journey is embedded in my mind and spirit. I know that someday I will reach the end of that trail too. In my preparation I will try to reach it in the time allotted and with dignity.

CHAPTER 22
LOOKING BACK

Speed is false on a well-used trail, winding and twisting like a giant snake through wild, green-infested woods. Thousands of rocks, each its own shape, color, and size, pass beneath the shoes of the loping runner, each rock gathering with others to form families huddled closely together.

The rotten log partially extends across the snake trail, altering speed to a standstill, forcing the body around a decaying mass of wood, now softened by its years of deadness and winter storms. The prone tree, once a majesty of the forest, crashed years ago, a fate of lightning, the logger's saw, or perhaps the wrath of age and inner decay.

A tiny channel among the rocks, dirt, and minute weeds and grasses, clumsily crosses the jagged path, a channel of the winter snow melt moisture, once churning in bubbling quickness, now gone to nothingness in the late summer's heat. The dead stream waits for rebirth, a new seed being planted from the deep winter snowfalls that will once more roar down the depths of the winding, twisting gully.

Suddenly around a corner, behind a giant boulder taller than a man, a remnant of some ancient landslide centuries old, an awesome vista of the canyons and peaks, thrusts itself at the eyes of the runner. Speed momentarily stops altogether for a quick side trip to take in the grandeur; now running on the trail becomes unimportant for a brief moment. Soft gentle breathing melts into the treetop music of the high breezes as the eyes accept with gentle respect the majesty of the land, its dash, its hopeful incongruity of jagged peaks and wayward canyons.

Time stops for a moment, really ceases to move for a few precious seconds of unity with some higher form of reality, the gut-sucking depth of a heavenly presence out here on a high mountain trail. Where did the trail come from? Has it always been here? Why does it go where it does? The unanswered questions rattle the brain to numbness, but the answers are really unimportant, for one doesn't need to question why. The trail, the beautiful path with a personality all its own, exists, and that is enough to the trail runner.

I become a different person on the trails, someone special to myself and in my relationship to my creator. Before doing the Western States I set forth my reasons for doing it and how I would approach the race both physically and mentally. Now many months after my accomplishment I can stand back and look at my effort a little more objectively. My main question is what did I gain from doing the event that I could never gain from doing anything else? The impact of the race on my life has been very powerful, both from the reactions of my friends and to my inner self.

Twenty years after the event I continue to feel the impact of the race. Today as I venture out on a trail nothing much has really changed. I still feel the power of the path that winds along to some far away destination. The pull of its inner spirit still draws me forth, only much more slowly now as my aging legs can no longer take the pace of a ultrarunner. Instead I walk aggressively and occasionally break into a slow trot, if only for a minute or two. As the trail takes me to its destination, I understand completely that the journey is much slower now, but that with the patience of life I will reach its end in good stead.

On the pure obvious level of reactions from others, my life has changed. I enjoy the recognition from others, and although it can become old telling the same stories to different people, I realize people really enjoy hearing an impossible story from someone who has gone through it. It is difficult for me to know what their conception of the race must be, except to try to remember my own ideas about the event when I first heard someone who had run it tell about it. At that time I could barely conceive of how it was possible to finish such an event, so I can understand someone's awe when I am asked about my experience.

Twenty years later no one brings it up any more. Most of the people who were near me then have already heard about it or are no longer a major part of my life. When I mention the race, most people look at me now and their looks tell me that they either don't believe me or that if it is true, they probably don't have the capacity to understand and so don't pursue the topic further. These are people who don't run or even walk much, and since I don't run much like I used to, they find the running of a 100 mile race inconceivable and incomprehensible. It no long matters that they don't really care to hear about it. What I do understand is that I still experience the feeling whenever I desire, only on a smaller scale whenever I take a short mountain hike along a gentle winding trail, above some crashing river rushing down over the rocks directly below. My experience never ends.

Yet having done the race, I realize that in actuality completing the event isn't as difficult as one might imagine, although there is no doubt that it means the bringing together of all the best a person has to offer both physically and mentally. Completing the race doesn't take a superman; it does, however, take super dedication and commitment to train oneself to the ultimate peak in preparation. Before I even considered trying the event, it just seemed too far away and difficult to ever attempt. Now I can see it objectively as a very difficult endurance event that is within the realm of any endurance athlete's capabilities if he or she so desires to commit the body and soul to it.

I no longer today commit myself to such races as the body refuses to respond to the challenge. However, my commitment to other causes is as strong as ever. I find I do not fear taking on challenges of all kinds, some of them mental and others physical. After all, isn't that what living a fulfilled life is all about? If I don't take on a variety of challenges in my life, I become a walking vegetable, seemingly content on the surface, but underneath my roots slowly rotting away. Whether it is the simple act of reading a book or the challenge of taking on the steep pitch of a black diamond ski run, I live because of these challenges. The trail is never smooth or it becomes a highway or road. Life is never or should it be smooth, for when it does and challenges cease to exist for me, life becomes meaningless and I will stop pursuing the end of my trail and simple die.

I often wonder why I want to do the event again, knowing I have nothing to prove and also knowing that I might invite failure. First of all, the time I spent out there during the race itself was one of the most fun and exciting days in my life. That's right; the running of the race was almost a heavenly experience. Yes, I would like to do it again, to experience the tremendous satisfaction and sensation of being out there on the course. During the moments of the race, I was my own hero, but I was also considered something very special in the eyes of the world on that very special day.

Today 20 years after the event it is still fun to go out on the trails and go for a long hike, perhaps with a few steps of slow running thrown in. I did do the race again and I did many others before I finally figured out that my body was no longer capable of doing them. Yet my slower and shorter jaunts out into the wilderness and even the tamer journeys along trails in safer environs are still fun and pure joy. Every time I go I can still feel a little of that heavenly experience.

Gordy Ainsleigh, the pioneer of the race, said it best when he noted that during the rest of the year away from the race, he is just another ordinary person, but that during the week and day of the race, he becomes a legend. Where else can one become a legend during one day, even more so by finishing the race? I remember the admiration and almost envy I held for every finisher of the race the year before I ran it. I wanted to be part of that legend, to be a finisher, to once in my life be able to say that I reached back and prepared to the very best of my ability to accomplish an almost unreachable goal, and then topped it off by reaching that goal.

Do I consider myself a legend? Of course, the answer is an emphatic no. Certain people in our world become legends, such people as actors and great athletes. Others become legends in many different fields, such as politics, television personalities, music, art, and medicine. Often these people let it go to their heads and actually believe that they are special beyond any other person of normal means and ability. Some of them are completely engrossed in their celebrity status, and often use this status to promote unpopular personal causes, incorrectly believing that they have superior powers and beliefs over anyone else.

In the long run of life, doing this race didn't make me a legend or even anyone special. All it did was confirm to me that we all have our own specials paths in life, and that these paths are important to us. My path is no more important or better than yours. All that is important is that it is what I choose to do with my life. We may cross paths in our journeys, but yours is just as special as mine. I am no better or no worse than anyone else. If the trail could speak, it would probably tell me to enjoy every little nuance along the journey, not to rush it, and to keep on forging ahead around the next bend.

Today the author enjoys hiking on trails around Mt. Shasta.

THE EPILOGUE
SPECIAL PEOPLE

The successful completion of this race 20 years ago could not have been done without the help of some special people who spent extra time to see me through the event and also provided me encouragement before and during the event. Some of them I don't see much anymore. Others I see occasionally and wish it could be more often. With one person I still remain in close touch. I would like to first mention four of those special people and the impacts they had on my success in the race.

David Calderon was the first of our inner group to run the Western States and he completed it under 24 hours. I was his pacer on that attempt, and I didn't do the job as completely as I should have, unable to complete the last part due to stomach problems of my own. His courage and determination on the run, his dedication to his training, and the glow and pleasure he received from winning his buckle, showed me that I could earn one of those symbols of achievement.

David was an accomplished marathoner, having run in the 2:30's. He later completed another Western States and other ultras. In preparation for his race and mine the next year, we trained together many times and ran many races together, and he had always been a friend to all our running club members, even the slower ones like myself. Whenever the training became a bore or tough, or the task seemed impossible just before the race, thinking of his accomplishments and character gave me inspiration to continue with the mission. On race day he was there as a member of my crew.

Rob Stephenson was my pacer, eager to do the job correctly, and he went out with the attitude that he would positively get me in under 24 hours if he had to drag me. He didn't have to do that, but he verbally and emotionally pulled me during my lowest and darkest moments. An outstanding runner in his own right, we ran one 50 miler together and did several other training runs, and I knew we were right on key with each other. He talked to me during the run, helped me through some trouble spots, encouraged me, jumped on me a couple of times when I wanted to rest a little more than I should, yet was patient with my cursing and grumbling when I was fighting the pain of the long miles.

A couple of years later Rob was accepted to run the Western States, but an injury he sustained during a 50 miler kept him from the starting line. He never did return to the race. Today we remain close friends and occasionally find ourselves out on some shorter race course together. Even now, as he did many years ago, he finishes far ahead of me by the end of the race.

Roger Sebert was my running guru friend, my sometimes training partner who would outrun me in a race and be out of sight after a few minutes. He was a frequent age group winner in all kinds of distances. He too was accepted in the Western States the same time as I was, and he completed the race in 22 hours and 30 minutes, about what I expected from the first try by such an outstanding and determined runner.

We went together to several training runs and a couple of races to prepare for this race, and we had many hours to express our hopes and fears to each other during all the time we were together. Roger kept people loose with his off beat humor, but hearing his serious side, listening to his own fears of the race, his problems with training and injuries, and his trouble keeping himself mentally peaked for the race, made me realize that I wasn't the only one with these problems.

Finally there was Richard Rodriguez, my crew chief. Richard had crewed for David the year before, when none of us knew what we were doing. When he heard I was in the race, Richard enthusiastically volunteered to head my crew. What could I say but yes. This guy was a friend before and during the race, and his verbal encouragement at all the stops, his jokes, and his true concern for me always made me look forward to seeing him at the next crew access point. Richard too was an accomplished runner and completed many marathons and several ultras.

This guy went beyond the call of duty to organize virtually everything, leaving me more free time to train and to be able to concentrate on the race itself during race day. I didn't have to worry about something being forgotten or overlooked. Richard had it all together and told me to just go run. I will forever be in his debt for all the time he sacrificed just for me. It's not easy being a crew member; yet he did it with unbound, genuine enthusiasm.

I would like to also thank my other crew members Len Hansen, Paul Jaramillo, and Bob Kearney, as well as Roger's crew of Larry Nava, Jeff Pierce, and Louie Martin. All were fine runners as well. Jeff and Louie ran numerous ultramarathons during their running careers. A special thanks goes to one of my long time friends, teaching colleague, and my running inspiration, Frank Padilla, who also happened to be one the best age group runners in the state.

More thanks go out to special people who provided me encouragement and a place to stay during my runs in the Sacramento area. They include my cousins Helen Jean and Rich Reese and my aunt and uncle Irma and Eldee Wirth. Other people who encouraged me were my brother Ed, who also ran and did triathlons and his wife Hilda, my sister and brother-in-law Kathy and Mark Enea, my late father Sid Fischer and my mother Ellen Fischer, forever enthusiastic about whatever I did, two very active beautiful people who always had an unbound, positive outlook on life.

Between 1980 and the present I have participated in over 420 running events, including 35 marathons and 39 ultras. Anymore, I do about three or four races a year and only for fun. I keep hoping that I might do a few more than that in the future. Some of my PR's include 37:26 for the 10K, 1:26:22 for the half marathon, 3:06:10 for the marathon, 7:51 for 50 miles, and 110 miles for 24 hours. Today my PR's are only in my mind. I have the usual collection of T-shirts and today my silver belt buckle still rests on a shelf in my living room. I retired from teaching in 2000 and my main athletic goal nowadays is to take to the ski slopes at least 25 times every winter, where I am finding new trails to conquer.

ABOUT THE AUTHOR

John David Fischer was born and raised in Dunsmuir, California in 1942, near the slopes of Mt. Shasta, where he learned to ski as a teenager, and only steps from the Upper Sacramento River, one of the best trout fishing streams on the west coast. It was here that he developed his great love for the outdoors.

He attended Chico State University where he received his degree and teaching credential in English and Journalism. After one year of teaching he served three years in the Army, two of those in Alaska. He then taught high school English for 31 years in Visalia, California, where he also coached in the baseball and football programs. He retired in 2000, but continued as a volunteer football coach through the 2005 season.

The author fishing the Sacramento River.

Also known as J.D. or Dave by the people who know him well, Fischer took his first steps as a runner in 1979 and ran his first marathon in 1981. Over the next two decades he completed 35 marathons and 39 ultramarathons, including the Western States in 1986 and 1989. He no longer runs the longer distances, but occasionally runs slowly in the shorter events.

In retirement he has reverted back to his earlier loves. He loves to take long hikes, go alpine skiing at least 25 days a years, and still returns each summer to fly fish his beloved Upper Sacramento River. This account of his running adventure is his second book.